From Kansas
to
Kilimanjaro

FROM KANSAS TO KILIMANJARO

A memoir of a family that survived two World Wars and outwitted Russian espionage

DAVID A. EMERY, PHD

Industrial Psychologist

iUniverse, Inc.
Bloomington

From Kansas to Kilimanjaro
A Memoir of a Family That Survived Two World
Wars and Outwitted Russian Espionage

Maps by Roni Melikokis

iUniverse books may be ordered through booksellers or by contacting:

iUniverse
1663 Liberty Drive
Bloomington, IN 47403
www.iuniverse.com
1-800-Authors (1-800-288-4677)

ISBN: 978-1-4697-9485-3 (sc)
ISBN: 978-1-4697-9487-7 (e)
ISBN: 978-1-4697-9486-0 (dj)

Library of Congress Control Number: 2012906349

Printed in the United States of America

iUniverse rev. date: 6/6/2012

Contents

My Sincere Gratitude

For the IBM Corporation's support,

For the Ford Foundation's support
and trusting delegation of project particulars,

For all those British Tommies who boosted my
morale out there in the Libyan desert when
there wasn't a thing I could do for them.

FOREWORD

Nearing graduation from college in 1942, the author volunteered to drive an ambulance in the American field service and became attached to the British Eighth Army's lead tank brigade in North Africa. He helped save lives and nearly lost his own. Returning to finish his education, he became an industrial psychologist and family man. The Cold War brought him back to Africa with his family, where he became involved with the KGB, the CIA, and the FBI.

The author

RELATIVES MATTER

Rudolphus David Emery, my grandfather, was a contemporary of Abraham Lincoln for four years (Lincoln was killed in 1865). The temporal overlap may be trivial, but there were significant similarities in their lives.

Both spent most of their youth on farms in the Midwest. Both were avid readers and mostly self-educated. Both were tall and very strong. Both were politically liberal and lived by their principles. Finally, both earned lasting respect and admiration from those who knew them well.

My earliest memories of my grandfather go back to the years when my parents and I lived together with my grandparents in the big old house my grandfather built in Des Moines, Iowa. Most evenings after dinner, Grandpa moved into the study room, stoked and lit his pipe, lifted me up on his lap, and read from Rudyard Kipling's *Just So Stories*. Grandpa read *How the Elephant Got His Trunk* again and again because he knew it was my favorite.

As a young man, my grandfather was the teacher in a one-room schoolhouse. That meant not only teaching all grades from first through high school, but also collecting his students in a horse-drawn wagon each morning and bringing them to school. The farms were spread out with lots of open country between, so the parents insisted that my grandfather carry a loaded six-gun in case the students needed protection.

R. D. Emery (circa 1925)

Not too long after my grandfather took over as schoolmaster, a couple of the big high school boys decided to challenge the limits of his authority. As the pickup wagon bounced along, the boldest boy rudely addressed my grandfather by his nickname, "Dolph, we don't think you even know how to use that gun." My grandfather just kept on driving without making any response. A little farther along their route, he saw a prairie chicken perched on a mound at a distance well beyond reasonable target range. Cocking and raising the big revolver (which he had never fired), he squeezed off a shot that blasted the chicken away in a cloud of feathers. Grandpa never had any disciplinary problems or disrespectful comments after that.

Grandfather's Wedding Day

Grandpa met and courted Anna Mulkey, who lived with her parents in a sod house on their farm west of Norton, Kansas. My grandfather roomed in Norton. The courtship was successful, and the wedding ceremony was to take place out on the farm. On the scheduled day, everything was ready for the celebration; Anna was in her wedding gown, but my grandfather didn't appear. In desperation, my grandmother-to-be climbed to the top of the windmill in her wedding gown to see if Rudolphus was in sight on the road from Norton. He was!

When Grandpa finally arrived, he was flushed with embarrassment and humbly apologized. He had been ready early, picked up a book so as not to arrive too early, gotten involved in the book, and lost track of time.

My grandparents had three children: my father and his two younger sisters. To support his growing family, Grandfather went to work as an insurance salesman for the Great Western Life Insurance Company in Des Moines, Iowa. The market for life insurance in Iowa was mostly limited to city dwellers at that time, because the state population of farmers was only accessible by unpaved mud roads. So Grandpa bought a Model T Ford and drove out where no life insurance salesman had ventured. He also developed a low-pressure sales approach that opened up the life insurance market. His method was to drive along until he saw a farmer working a field, pull over by the fence, and just sit there. Invariably, the farmer's curiosity led him to come over by his fence. Greetings led to discussion about the weather, which led to speculation about crop productivity, which led to concerns about what might happen to threaten the welfare of the farmer's family, which led to the desirability of insuring the life of the man upon whom the family depended.

Grandfather sold more life insurance in Iowa than anyone thought was possible. He was soon promoted to teach other salesmen his method, and ultimately he became vice president of the company. Only inside political games kept him from becoming president. That was a disappointment, which Grandpa dealt with by retiring and buying 160 acres of land in the foothills of Colorado. He christened it The Wilds because it was beyond the end of the local county road, populated only by pines, aspen, and small wildlife.

My grandfather, with the help of a hired man, built a large log cabin by a creek and a barn for horses and cleared a field for crops and pasture. They also built a sawmill to cut lumber and fenced in much of the property. It was here that I and some cousins spent summers and learned how to build road, repair fence, service the light plant, and help with other odd jobs. I also learned some gymnastics and a little basic karate from one of our hired men, who thought it might come in handy some day. As time would tell, he was positively prescient.

One winter, during the school year, the big old log cabin caught fire and burned to the ground. My grandparents had to drive into Denver late in the night and stay with relatives. The next morning, at my grandmother's urging, they drove back up to The Wilds and began cleaning up the ashes and remains of the fire.

Author at The Wilds, age thirteen

They immediately began preparations for building a new larger cabin out of stone. The living room fireplace in the new cabin could take a six-foot log, uncut! The hearthstone was a single granite rock nine feet long, five feet wide, and three feet thick. We worked that huge boulder down from above and into position using rollers, levers, ropes and pulleys, skids, crowbars, picks, shovels, a hired man, and several relatives. We did it in a day with no injuries, very few arguments, and a great sense of accomplishment.

Years later, my grandfather died in his sleep. When my grandmother turned to him in the morning, he had a smile on his face.

FIRST LOVE

During my summers at the The Wilds before Grandfather passed away, I often went along with our hired man to get lumber and other building supplies in Evergreen. When I was sixteen, I was sometimes sent down to Evergreen alone with the truck and a shopping list. I enjoyed driving the truck and seeing how far I could make it back up Willmont Hill before having to double-clutch down into second gear. I was also on the lookout for a girl I had noticed with flaming red hair and a face and figure like Ginger Rogers.

Finally, I got my nerve up and, even though only dressed in dungarees and an undershirt, parked the loaded truck so I could cross over to where she was walking.

"Please excuse me," I said, "my name is David Emery, and I have been wanting to meet you."

"I think I know who you are," she replied with a smile. "My name is Georgia Goodrich. I'm just walking back to my home over there [nodding to the combined home and real estate agency office building near the edge of Bear Creek]."

"May I call and maybe visit you sometime?" I asked.

"Yes, you may. Do you have our number? It's my mother's agency."

Her voice was neither high nor low, just even and warm. I nodded, elated, and turned back to the truck. I felt like skipping and cheering but restrained myself to a steady stroll back to the truck. We exchanged waves and smiles as I started up.

We filled the rest of the summer with good times together. Often, I drove down to meet Georgia at her home. We would walk by the creek or sit in the bench swing together on her porch. Once when I was skipping stones out onto the smooth water nearby, I mistakenly hooked a flat rock that spun off and hit Georgia behind her left ear. It made a deep cut that bled profusely. Georgia didn't cry or even complain as her mother and I took care of the cut. I felt horrible!

Sometimes, Mrs. Goodrich would bring Georgia up to The Wilds. Mrs. Goodrich would visit with Grandmother while Georgia and I took long hikes around our property. Once I even lugged my portable Victrola with several records up the steep climb to the top of Alligator Rock, the highest peak on our property. Georgia's favorite song was a sentimental ballad called "Music, Maestro Please." I liked Latin music like La Cumparsita, La Cucaracha, and Cuban Pete.

We never felt a lack of things to talk about, probably because for me, and I think for Georgia as well, just being together in that beautiful environment was emotionally fulfilling.

The old adage "When there's a will, there's a way" seemed to apply to us. On two occasions when no car was available, I ran, trotted, and strode the six miles from The Wilds to Georgia's home. It was quite a workout, but my spirits were so high from seeing Georgia that the return trip was no problem.

A few times, we had more conventional dates. I took Georgia to Eddie Otts's nightclub on the waterfront of the big reservoir above Evergreen. Once, I took her to the Brown Palace Hotel in Denver for cocktails and dinner. Our favorite drink was Gin Alexander (we never had more than two). We also went to the big amusement park in Denver and rode the roller coaster.

On our last evening together before I returned to Des Moines for school, we danced at Eddie Otts's and then drove up Cub Creek to the Brook Forest Inn for a final Alexander followed by relaxation in a swing built for two on the terrace. It was a clear, mild moonlit night, and we soon wrapped ourselves into a heavy hugging, kissing, caressing session that drove me up such a crescendo of passion I burst out in a groan, "If I were more of a man, Georgia, I'd just take you!"

Georgia smiled up at me and replied, "That's just our problem, David. You're already too much of a man!" I think it was her calm humor and reminder of possible consequences that enabled me to cool it enough to keep my control.

We subsided into a review of our life plans for our short and long term together. First, Georgia would return to Texas to finish high school while I went on to college and medical school. As soon as Georgia graduated from her private school, we would be married and live together while I finished my medical training. A few years after that, we would consider starting a family. We both wanted to enjoy several years with just the two of us before taking on the responsibility and limitations of child care.

Cloudburst over Bear Creek Canyon

Two days after my return to Des Moines, I was alone at home when the front doorbell rang. I came down from my room and opened the door to a Western Union delivery man. I accepted the telegram and didn't open it until he left. The telegram was from my cousin in Denver. It read, "Georgia Goodrich and her mother killed in Bear Creek Canyon flash flood while returning from Denver."

In a state of extreme shock, I ran back upstairs to my bedroom and danced slowly around as if with Georgia. I kept doing that until my grandmother came home (my parents were away). Grandmother tried to comfort me, but nothing helped until she offered to pay for a trip to Colorado for me if I would like to go back there and return before school started. I accepted immediately and packed a few clothes and my Victrola with a few records.

A cousin met me at the Denver station and took me up to The Wilds. The next morning, the first thing I did was to take the Victrola and records and hike up to Alligator Rock where Georgia and I used to climb and play our music. After a while, I just came back down.

Later, I heard that Georgia and her mother had been shopping in Denver for Georgia's return to school in Texas. They were caught while driving back up Bear Creek Canyon by a six-foot wall of water that came crashing down at an estimated forty miles per hour, sweeping along rocks, trees, and masses of debris in the oncoming headwall. Nothing was found of the Goodriches' Buick or its contents except one of the license plates.

The tragedy of Georgia Goodrich left me in a state of shock. I loved Georgia without reservation and planned to spend the rest of my life with her.

I returned to Des Moines immediately, not wanting to attend any public services. Years later, I did visit relatives in Denver again. My cousin drove me back up to The Wilds just to have a look around.

At first, it looked as beautiful as ever, but when we stopped in front of the great old cabin, a very tough-looking, heavyset, middle-aged woman stepped out of the porch door, put fists on her hips, and asked us what we wanted.

When we explained we just wanted to see the place once more because we used to spend summers there, she sort of snorted, "Well, if I ever tried to visit all the places I've lived in … well!" Then she just stood and stared.

We took the hint and left. My cousin said to me, "I guess what I heard is true. After Uncle Dolph died, Aunt Anna sold the place for seven thousand dollars, and The Wilds became a transfer point for drug runners. The isolation with access from Brook Forest on one end and Evergreen on the other probably made it ideal for storage and, if needed, escape."

Grandparents Rudolphus D. Emery and Anna Mulkey Emery

Anna Mulkey Emery

My grandmother was a remarkable woman, both before and after my grandfather's death. Besides the customary cooking, dishwashing, and house cleaning, she put in and cared for a vegetable garden, patched our clothing, made quilts and dresses for the women in the family, and every fall season "put up" many large jars of preserves so we would have our own vegetables and fruits through the winter.

Whenever Grandma had a sewing project, she would let me get down under her old Singer sewing machine and push the treadle that powered the machine above. This made her sewing more complicated, but she knew I liked the feeling of making the machine work, so she let me go ahead while she moderated my energetic action by keeping one hand on the flywheel above.

Grandmother was also very brave. Once, when she got her right hand caught between the rollers of the ringer on our old washing machine down in the basement, the first anyone else knew about it was when my mother and I saw Grandma coming slowly up the basement stairs, she was pulling the skin of her third finger on her right hand back down on that raw, exposed finger. She quickly explained what had happened while she continued to slip the skin back in place. Grandmother didn't even want us to call Dr. Saunders. Fortunately, the finger healed completely.

My grandfather and grandmother were the core of our entire family. Whenever some relative needed financial help, they turned to my grandfather. Whenever the problem was some emotional crisis, they sought understanding and advice from Grandmother. Together, these two caring people gave support to family members located in Iowa, Nebraska, Kansas, Colorado, and beyond.

In only one case that I know of was the care misguided with serious consequences. The care I have in mind was overprotection and lack of discipline in my grandmother's treatment of my father. Amos Barton Emery, my grandparents' only son, had some behavioral characteristics not uncommon in firstborn males: excessive aggressiveness toward a younger sister, unreasonable resistance to cooperation in mildly unpleasant chores, and refusal to accept limitations imposed by authorities.

An example of this negativism, and my grandmother's excessive tolerance in dealing with it, was noted by other family members and never forgotten. It was a standard practice after meals for the children to pitch in with the washing and drying of the dishes. Amos and his younger sisters, Grace and Ruth, were all involved and more or less rotated the several necessary tasks. Actually, it was not an equal division. When a visiting relative asked Grandma why Amos never dried the silverware, Grandma explained, "Oh, Amos doesn't dry silver!"

Amos Emery, author's father

Amos Emery, 1916

Alice Cusson Emery 1918.

Alice Cusson Emery, 1918, author's mother

How My Parents Met

My father was a "natural" for war in the skies. His vision was excellent, especially his depth perception; his coordination was quick and accurate; his attitude was highly aggressive; even his limited height was a plus in the cockpit. He should have been a fighter pilot, but the De Havillands the United States trained in and shipped to France during World War I were used mostly for observation of troop movements on the ground.

On leave in Paris, Amos met Alice. Alice was wearing an armband that was issued to bilingual Parisian women indicating their capability as translators. Utilizing that as a pretext, my father-to-be asked my mother where he could buy some bread. They were married a month later.

Alice turned out to be an energetic, stimulating, granddaughter of a countess, whose husband, the Count, had been treasurer to Louis XIV. The king had praised the count when the count retired with these words: "You are the person who has handled the most of my money and kept the least." Quite a catch to show off to the folks back home in Des Moines! More than that, it was Alice whose French lessons years later kept our credit afloat during the Great Depression (despite a lot of unforgiveable behavior on Amos's part).

Mother was a relentless teacher. Every weekday at five o'clock, her call for me to come home for my hour of piano practice could be heard throughout the neighborhood. She failed to make a pianist out of me, but my mother's pacifism and "one-world" perspective did make me an ardent pacifist and were positive factors in my choice of Haverford College, a Quaker school with a reputation of high academic standards.

I was in for a surprise at Haverford. As the male with the top grades in my high school in Des Moines, I was in danger of failing by midterm at Haverford. I was saved by my mother, who came East, rented an apartment at the edge of our campus, and drilled me daily in my French and German lessons. I passed midterms.

Author with mother

Amos and author, circa 1922

College Choice and Study Priorities

I majored in philosophy at Haverford College because I thought philosophy was where I would find answers to questions I had been wondering about for years.

- Why do people feel and act the way they do?
- What really motivates humans?
- How do motives change or not change?

After a year as a philosophy major, I decided none of the philosophers I had studied really provided satisfactory answers to my questions. How about psychologists?

I arranged to take an introductory psychology course over at Swarthmore under Wolfgang Köhler, the great Gestalt psychologist. When asked questions about motivation, Köhler readily admitted that neither philosophers nor psychologists really knew much about motivation. Köhler had studied physics and understood scientific method, which he felt was lacking in the thinking of psychologists like Freud, Jung, and Adler. In Köhler's view, these "authorities" and their followers were presenting unproven theories as established facts. For his part, Köhler preferred to apply the scientific method to elements of human behavior that could be observed systematically and tested in repeatable experiments. For that reason, his work dealt mostly with perception.

I liked this and later became Köhler's assistant in research on satiation effects in human depth perception.

PACIFIST GOES TO WAR

In 1942, during my final year at Haverford, it seemed obvious that the United States would become involved in the war with Japan and Germany. This forced me to make some decisions about my future because I had been thinking and writing about pacifism for several years. The root of my feelings was that although I had shot rats, chipmunks, and squirrels, I absolutely could not imagine raising a rifle and squeezing off a shot at a human unless he was clearly trying to kill me.

With this attitude and my view of international developments, I searched for some way out of the probable conflict. Though I had been thinking, talking, and writing like a conscientious objector, I could not deny the necessity of stopping Hitler and Tojo. And I admit, I was also concerned for my own life.

I found a way: the American Field Service based in New York City had sent ambulances and drivers to France in World War I and was now providing ambulances with volunteer drivers to serve wherever needed in World War II. Haverford, with its Quaker background, was ready to release seniors who volunteered for the AFS from their final semester to graduate in absentia without taking the dreaded final comprehensive exams in their major area. I'll admit that final escape clinched the deal for me. My major department head had liked the papers I wrote, but the idea of submitting to comprehensive questioning about the concepts of all the philosophers I had studied was mind-boggling.

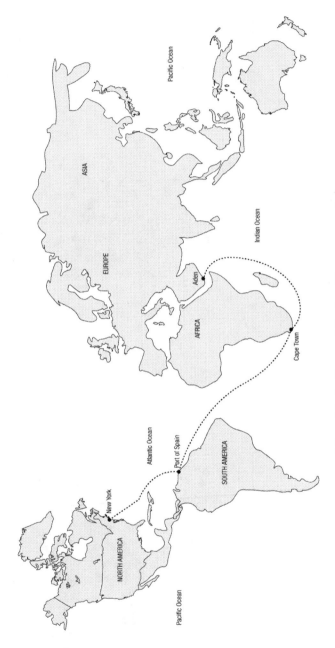

New York, Port of Spain, Capetown, Aden

Ambulance Driver in North Africa

The first leg of our trip to Africa was from New York to Port of Spain, the harbor of Trinidad. Our ship, the Selandia, was an elegant thirteen-thousand-ton Danish passenger-freighter. We sailed in early June 1942, paused briefly in Port of Spain, and headed out in a zigzag pattern across the South Atlantic. Our devious course was due to reports of German submarines operating in that area. Determined not to go down with the ship, I set up my sleeping bag on the top deck next to one of the lifeboats. In my fantasy, the state freestyle champion of Iowa would either swim some incredible distance to a foreign shore, or at least be picked up by the attacking sub's crew.

We had two performances to break the monotony of the long trip to Capetown. The first was a wrestling match between me and Pete Goldberg, a young man from Seattle. Pete outweighed me by twenty pounds and knew how to use his weight. It was a long match that Pete finally won by sitting on me when I was completely exhausted. After the match, we became lasting friends.

As the Selandia zigzagged on toward Capetown, some members of our group were secretly working on a musical comedy. It had everything: plot, characters, piano accompaniment, and loaded with humor. The characters were mostly women in striking costumes. In fact, as a member of the audience, it struck me that the whole show was primarily a vehicle for the gays in our company to express themselves in clothing, language, and mannerisms they normally suppressed. It also reinforced my impression that there were at least as many individuals in our company whose primary motivation to join the field service was more to escape something than to contribute something. We had escapees from failing careers, from limiting social norms, from being forced to do things they abhorred, from just plain boredom, and to avoid comprehensive exams!

The relevant question here was if they would make good ambulance drivers. Most of them did, because they would be caught in situations where their help was needed, and they were more or less constrained to give it.

Capetown

Capetown, South Africa, is one of the most beautifully situated cities in the world. As our ship approached, the forefront of beaches and the backdrop of mountains framed the city like a perfect molding of the inanimate physical and animate living elements of nature.

We received a royal welcome in Capetown beginning with invitations into houses and a club where we met people who knew about our mission and were expecting our arrival. I dined with a young widow whose husband had been on a ship sunk by the Germans. She didn't say much about it but clearly was still suffering from the loss. I admired her willingness to socialize with other young men caught up in the war.

Taking the "trams" (streetcars) to get around in Capetown, I was startled to see the extent of racial segregation everywhere. The blacks not only were confined to the rear of the trams, they had to wait for the trams in a separate space from white people. I concluded this was done both to separate the blacks from the whites and to make sure all the white people could board before any blacks did. If the trams were full, the blacks got left behind. No wonder rebellion was coming!

Capetown to Aden

The final ocean leg of our ambulance company's trip to Africa was done in a large former ocean liner that had been converted into a troop transport. Cabins originally designed for two had been remodeled to sleep sixteen, with no additional plumbing. This was tolerable, until the ptomaine poisoning hit.

We were in the Red Sea, about level with Madagascar, when something our mess had for dinner made most of us simultaneously nauseous and diarrheic.

"Simultaneously" in this case means we all got sick at the same time, and we all needed to vomit and have fluid bowel movements at the same time. One didn't know which way to face the plumbing, if the plumbing were available. Need I say more? It was much more painful than whatever most of us would experience at the hands of the enemy. In fact, rumors of sabotage were heard on several levels of the ship. Cooks were warned to stay out of sight.

It was hard to imagine the pain would pass, or that the mess could ever be cleaned up, but it did and it was, and most of us were eating again during the following day. Youth is resilient, and we were getting excited about getting to port and on up to the desert where the British Eighth Army had finally stopped Rommel's advance.

We were trucked from the Port of Aden to El Tahag, a vast marshalling area of flat desert west of Cairo. The whole landscape, as far as we could see, was dotted with encampments and military equipment. We were told there were two purposes for our being there: first, to screen us to see who was fit to work in this kind of environment; and second, to familiarize us with our vehicle and its maintenance. We were told it was expected that up to one-third of us would have to be returned because of "sandfly fever," a desert dysentery that infects most people when they enter areas like the one we were in but is permanent in some as long as they remain in the desert. Fortunately, most of our company was able to stay. I wondered whether our bout with ptomaine had left us with antibodies that protected us from sandfly fever. Personally, I never suffered any stomach upset during the remainder of my stay in Africa.

We had some time to ourselves during this "shakedown" period which I used to explore Cairo and go to a small beach on the Suez

Canal. Out in the canal, an old yacht about eighty feet long lay at anchor. Inquiring, I learned that it belonged to Farouk, king of Egypt since 1936.

There was only a weak current in the canal, so I swam out to the yacht and hand-over-handed up a heavy rope hanging down from a protruding beam. I went aboard and, seeing no one, walked back to the stern past the above-deck cabin, around the stern to the port side, and started forward along that side when I heard something behind me. Looking back, I saw two large Egyptians dressed like cooks walking toward me. One of them carried a heavy long, saberlike knife. They weren't smiling, and I didn't wait to see what they wanted. I ran on forward, across the bow, over to the rail, and dove for some underwater swimming and full speed freestyle back to the beach. Some girls were sitting there watching and shaking their heads. I headed back to camp, feeling cocky and lucky.

Author in his Ambulance truck

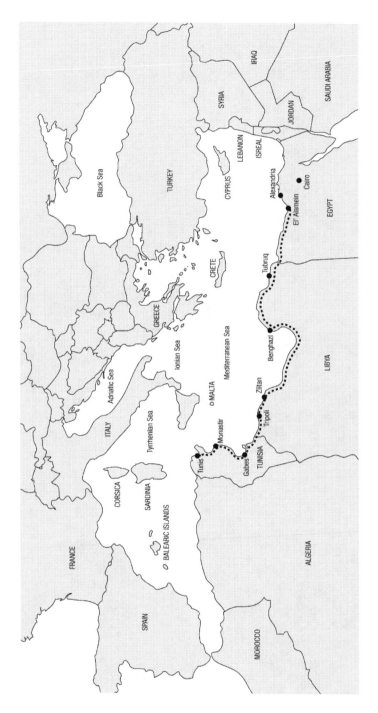

Aden to Cairo to El Alamein and points west.

El Alamein

My work as an ambulance driver began at El Alamein, where the British Eighth Army had set up a long barrier stretching from the shore of the Mediterranean Sea thirty-five miles down to an impassable badland depression in the desert. This barrier and probably the length of their supply lines had stopped the previously unstoppable German army of Field Marshal Erwin Rommel.

The British barrage in the night previous to the Eighth Army advance was incredible. It looked like a solid band of low-level lightning extending from the ground up to about one thousand feet and stretching from as far to the left and to the right as you could see. The noise of the cannons was never intermittent, just a constant loud rumble.

About an hour after the barrage began, some of our ambulances, including mine, were ordered to go forward along a track to an LAD (light aid division). We did this in a convoy with blinding dust until we were stopped. Soon, stretcher bearers brought wounded soldiers and loaded them (four stretchers to an ambulance). We were directed back to a CCS (casualty clearing station) where other stretcher bearers unloaded our ambulances, told us to wait, and soon returned the empty stretchers.

Sex in the Desert

Several days of routine transporting of wounded followed as the British began the drive westward against the Germans. I found the supply of bread, canned beef, sweetened condensed milk, wine, and tea I had accumulated very convenient as I occasionally was out of reach of our company mess.

Late on one of those evenings, I had just finished eating and "brewing up" my tea on my little primus stove when I felt like I was not alone. Peering out into the darkness, I could just make out a semicircle of Arabs about fifteen feet away, all facing me. I immediately took out the Beretta automatic (I had traded a motorcycle I repaired for it) and ostentatiously put it down close at hand. As I did that, the Arab in the middle of the group walked slowly toward me, miming that he would like some tea.

I gave him my cup (thereby occupying at least one of his hands) and put tea and hot water in it. He indicated he would like sugar so I offered some. He took several spoonfuls, gave it a stir, and chugalugged the whole mug. Then he reached into the fold at the level of his belt, and I quickly grabbed the Beretta. He hesitated then slowly extracted a small bottle from his waistband, opened the top, placed a finger on top, upended the bottle a moment, and reached over to touch his fingertip on my mustache. Then he nodded and withdrew. The others followed him, and I was left alone. I turned in, noting the perfumelike bouquet coming from my mustache. I slept soundly for a while, and then an amazing thing happened; still sleeping, I was launched into an incredible series of romantic dreams.

Obviously, the Arab had given me an olfactory aphrodisiac. I had never heard of such a thing and wondered if it were common in some parts of the world. One thing is for sure: if I could get the formula for that elixir, I could become a multi–multi–multi–whatever!

Back to Reality

Back to reality, I had a quick breakfast and continued on my way toward the front line. I hadn't gone far when a tall British officer flagged me down and asked for a ride back to his unit. Of course, I welcomed him in and got moving. After we had gone a mile or so, my passenger asked, "Does this vehicle have four-wheel drive?" I proudly assured him it did. He was silent for a while after that then turned toward me and said, "Driver, how would you like to be attached to the Notts?"

Noting the look of puzzlement on my face, the officer said indignantly, "The Nottingham Sherwood Rangers tank brigade, driver! I am the colonel's medical officer! Our brigade is the leading unit of the Eighth Army strike against Rommel."

I was impressed and took a closer look at his uniform. He was a captain all right, and probably a doctor. The idea of being right up there at the front was appealing to me, especially since the alternative seemed to be just back and forth, back and forth, hauling wounded between medical facilities when it was my turn, spending most of my time just waiting. So I told the captain I was interested. After a few minutes, our road passed near a cluster of tents. The captain said, "Stop and wait here, driver, while I see if I can make some arrangements." I did as I was told, and the captain strode off toward the encampment. He was gone about half an hour and returned to announce, "It's all arranged, driver. You will be attached to me. Now we go forward to the Notts."

(Parenthetically, let me tell you that about a month later, after I was no longer with the captain of his Notts, I found out that he had not made any arrangements of any kind except to have a cup of tea with some other officers. Consequently for weeks, field service headquarters had me down as missing in action. My parents were terribly worried. When I learned about all this, I concluded that the doctor's motive for the fraud was to have his own four-wheel transport and evacuation unit available whenever needed. By the time the truth came out, I already knew my doctor was a fraud in a much more serious way, but more about that later.)

My first night with the Notts was a real baptism of fire. We caught up with the tank brigade in a small depression where they were taking heavy fire. One of the tanks had been hit and was beginning to smoke. I drove nearby, jumped out, and ran over to the smoking tank in time to see one member of its crew struggling to get out of the turret. I helped him get free and walked him back to my ambulance. Then I headed back toward the tank. I didn't get far before I was stopped in my tracks by a ghastly sight. Coming slowly toward me were two soldiers holding their arms out in front of their bodies with what at first looked like gloves hanging down, inside out, held in place by their fingernails. There wasn't much light, but as they came closer I could see that what looked like partially removed gloves were actually their own skin, burnt from their exposed forearms down, hanging down and prevented from falling free by their fingernails.

I offered help, but they just shook their heads and walked on. I realized they were the remainder of the crew I had thought were dead inside the tank with the man in the turret. They seemed to know where they wanted to go, so I continued back to my ambulance, frustrated and sad at being unable to help them. It was my first face-to-face confrontation with some of the real horrors of war, and I'll never forget those poor, surprised looking young men.

HAVERFORD NEWS

Tuesday, January 12, 1943

Graduate Presented Citation For Bravery In Libyan Campaign

According to a Cairo dispatch from the New York Times, David A. Emery, a graduate of Haverford in 1942, has become a "daredevil of the desert" serving with the American Field Service in Libya. Last reported at Sirte with the British forces chasing Rommel out of Africa, Emery has been doing time and a "hero" overtime with three nations.

Commended by British officers for conspicuous bravery under fire, Emery rescued a British tank crew from their flaming steel wagon while under shell fire from the German artillery. Then, serving with the New Zealanders from "way down under," he and his Field Service crew were with the troops that swept around the German Flank to the sea, cutting them off.

A native of Des Moines, Iowa, Emery, while at college was a Philosophy major. In extra-curricular activities, he was a member of the Phil Club, the Service Project, and the Chemistry Club.

Digging My Grave?

When the Notts moved forward, I was told to stay put until I received further orders. When sunrise came, I was alone and not sorry for that. It looked like a chance to relax a little and regroup emotionally.

But that was not to be! Though the entire area around me was now clear of any men or equipment, I could hear shelling in the distance. It sounded like it came from the north, and as I continued to listen, it seemed to come closer. More careful listening convinced me that the enemy was doing what we called "area saturation" shelling, a tactic for eliminating any equipment following in support of our striking unit, the lead tanks.

Whatever, I didn't like it. It seemed to be moving steadily, area by area, in my direction. Had I not been ordered to "Hold your position, driver," I would certainly have prepared to relocate (to put it mildly), but I knew I was supposed to say where I was in case my ambulance was needed up front. So I immediately got my small spade out of the car and began digging myself a slit trench. The digging was not difficult, but the speed seemed essential. I made a fairly neat hole six feet long, two feet wide, and two feet deep. Testing for size, I found it a good fit: it was snug and allowed all of me to be a foot or more below ground level. The close fit seemed important in order to reduce the chances of being hit by flying shrapnel from a close strike.

It worked. I was all set should the shelling reach my area, which it did. My biggest problem was sustaining my sanity between the time I finished my trench and the time those gunners targeted my area. I needed distraction and found it by composing some appropriate lyrics to the popular song, "My Mommy Done Told Me." Here is what I came up with.

> A Tommy Done Told Me
> A Tommy done told me,
> Deep down in a slit trench,
> A Tommy done told me, Chum,
> I've been in the Big Do,
> Seen bags of the shit fly,
> But there is one thing I know:

36

I'm bloody well browned off,
There's fuck-all to do,
Way up in the blue,
With bombs in the night!

From Alex to Tobruk,
From Barci to Sirte,
Wherever those MEs play,
I've been in the Big Do,
Seen bags of the shit fly,
And there is one thing I know:
I'm bloody well browned off,
There's fuck-all to do,
Way up in the blue,
With bombs in the night!

Hear the Stukas whistle,
Better duck that missile,
Whooie, a Tommy done told me,
A whooie da whooie!
So hang onto your seat,
We're gonna retreat,
From bombs in the night!

Shortly after I completed my lyrics, the German-filled artillery went to work on "my" area. They were very thorough; leaving the area looking like it had been infested by a colony of giant ants. The hit closest to me splintered a former power line pole about twenty feet from my slit trench but left me unscathed. The noise and concussion sounded and felt like the world had blown up. How lucky can you get?

Eighth Army Advance

The Eighth Army under Montgomery moved steadily forward, forcing Rommel to retreat westward across Egypt into Libya. I was unable to keep up with the tanks because somewhere inside Libya, we came across a vertical drop in the desert floor that extended for miles both to the north and south. The tanks crossed the four- to six-foot drop by easing their front half out over the edge and slowly advancing the tank at a steep angle until all of it was down at the lower level. To avoid getting hung up on the edge with my ambulance, I backed off about one hundred feet and gunned the engine in four-wheel drive. I made it over the drop-off, but the landing broke both the Dodge's front springs. That left me limited to less than ten miles an hour mobility forward or backward and ended my usefulness to the Notts.

I was marooned out there in the desert for over a week when the repair unit of my ambulance company caught up with me. This was not a hardship, thanks to the supply of water, wine, and food I always carried in the ammo tin I had installed between the front seats of my ambulance. I had the primus cooker for brewing up, plenty of petrol on the roof rack, and a copy of War and Peace, which I had always intended to read. What better time than now, while a whole army was passing by me?

My only problem was there were so many interruptions. It seemed that every advancing unit had someone who wanted to help me, or at least find out what I was doing sitting out there in the Libyan desert reading Tolstoy.

As it turned out, this forced delay may have saved my life. One of my visitors brought the news that the colonel of the Notts had his head shot off by "friendly fire" as our brigade entered Tripoli. He had been riding in the lead tank and sitting, as usual, with his upper body sticking up out of the main turret. An example of bravery or foolhardiness? Perhaps I should learn from that!

Whatever, the military loses little time over selecting replacements, especially when a major advance is underway. As spearhead of the British Eighth Army, the Notts were pushing on up the northeast coast of Libya toward Tunis to form a pincer with American forces coming westward from Morocco.

Once my field service repair unit reached my area, my job was to get two replacement front springs, get them installed, and try to catch up with the Notts.

It took a week for everything I wanted to happen; I finished War and Peace, the AFS repair unit appeared, I was able to jack up the front end of my ambulance and remove the broken parts of both front springs and mount the replacements, and I found a place where other units had created a passable ramp. I was on my way!

Killer or CO?

I seemed to have a knack for getting into situations with ambiguous implications. One afternoon after a long drive in my recently repaired ambulance, I was awakened from a nap by the whine of a diving airplane. It was a Stuka making repeated vertical dives, releasing a bomb, then pulling up into a steep climb and firing down at us from the famous Stuka "sting in the tail" that the pilot aimed with mirrored gun sites. Sort of a nasty antipersonnel device.

I grabbed the Mauser rifle I had acquired, jumped under my ambulance, and squeezed off shots whenever I got a bead on the climbing plane. Everyone else in the area was doing the same thing, but I was the only ambulance around and my car had a large red cross on the roof. According to the Geneva Convention, ambulances were not supposed to be fired upon. American field service drivers all carried Geneva cards to prove their noncombatant citizen status. I failed to adhere to my legal status in this case. I felt an overwhelming impulse to try to hit back at the attacker, though I didn't have any basis for assuming he was targeting the ambulance.

I doubt that I actually hit the plane but something did. Its climb slowed, and smoke began to come out of the tail. The pilot bailed out and began to fall with his parachute lines trailing behind him. The parachute failed to open until he was only a few hundred feet above the ground.

I jumped into my ambulance, started the engine, and raced off in the direction of his fall. He was no longer in sight, but as I got closer, I saw him walking in my direction. I stopped the car, grabbed the keys, and jogged in his direction. He kept walking toward me, looking quite bedraggled as he got closer. Without any overt communication between us, he joined me and we walked together back to my ambulance. He got in the passenger seat, and I drove immediately to the medical station not far from us.

I parked about fifty yards from the reception tent, and we walked together toward the tent. Suddenly, we were both knocked down to the ground by three "Tommies" (British soldiers). I was furious and began cursing them as I got up. They remained silent, two of them holding the German down while the third held out a Luger pistol he had taken from the pilot. I shut up as I realized what had happened;

40

the Tommies had seen that the pilot carried a sidearm and weren't taking any chances as to what the pilot might do.

I departed, still stunned by the whole experience. At the beginning, I had wanted to see that dive bomber shot down and killed. Then when he was hit, I immediately wanted to help him if I could. Some sort of a paradox, or was it just that once the threat of him harming me disappeared my more humane motives took over?

Airman Contact # 2

My next experience with a pilot came at night with much greater difficulties and consequences. The Notts had momentarily halted their advance. Doctor Captain Young and I were bivouacked close to the lead tank with its new commander. I was hoping for a night's rest, but that was not to be.

We heard a plane that didn't sound like either a Junker or a Stuka come over at low altitude, and then quite suddenly the engine noise stopped. About fifteen minutes later, two heavy breathing stretcher bearers came into our camp with a blanket-covered body on their stretcher. We quickly set up two ammo boxes so they could deposit their load. As they did this, a man's head raised slightly near one end of the stretcher, looked around, and dropped back on the canvas without making a sound.

One of the stretcher bearers mumbled, "Medium bomber plane, South African pilot, shot up by an 88, shell went through his leg, brought plane down and saved his crew. Tough bloke." Then the stretcher bearers left.

Doctor Captain Young pushed the blanket off to expose the left leg. It was crudely bound below the thigh with blood-soaked bandaging, which the doctor removed. The deep, ugly wound was not bleeding heavily, but the slight angle of bend at this midthigh location clearly indicated a broken thigh bone. Captain Young opened his doctor's bag, extracted his scalpel, and began cutting away loose flesh from around the edges of the wound. Watching the procedure closely, I noticed that the doctor seemed to be slowing down and wiping perspiration from his brow. Soon he turned to me, held out the scalpel, and said, "Here, driver. Carry on."

I was shocked and furious. In our briefings back at El Tahag, we had been told repeatedly that what seriously wounded men needed most was to be treated for shock, and that what helped reduce shock most was prompt removal from the location of the disaster. Maybe I was being unfair to Captain Young, but it seemed to me his chief interest was in being awarded a decoration for major medical performance under battlefield conditions.

In any case, this was not the time to probe the doctor's motivation. I took the scalpel and went to work on that leg. There was no bone left to deal with where the shell had passed through, but I was amazed at how difficult ligaments and muscle are to sever, even with a scalpel. I was also surprised that the man on the stretcher, who was clearly conscious, never cried out.

I sprinkled sulfa powder to limit infection and bandaged everything as best I could. Finally, I rigged a tourniquet around the leg between the wound and his hip, making a mental note to release the pressure occasionally if I was with the patient for long. That turned out to be the case. The nearest LAD was about twenty-five kilometers south of us with minefields along the way and no established track to follow. No headlights could be used because the enemy was too near. So I set forth with my patient bundled up in one of my stretchers and the heater on. I had been given a compass bearing and knew how to confirm my heading by periodically walking out in front of the ambulance with my prismatic compass (necessary to avoid compass distortion caused by the car's idling engine). I was not concerned about driving at night without headlights since I knew from experience that on a clear night like this one, there is always enough light from the stars to see large objects on the horizon. On this particular night there would be no moon for most of the night, which was fortunate because this meant my ambulance was unlikely to be seen from a distance.

The trip was uneventful. My patient was so quiet I had to check once in a while to make sure he was still alive. When I had driven the twenty-five kilometers (a little over 15 1/2 miles) I stopped, left the engine idling, and walked out as far as I dared without losing sight of the ambulance. Then I returned to the car and walked out again at a forty-five-degree angle from my first excursion. I did this until I had covered quite a wide area with my wheel-spoke search pattern.

Having seen no sign of the LAD on this first search, I drove on a short distance and repeated my wheel-spoke pattern. No luck. I kept on until I had reached a point well beyond the twenty-five-kilometer distance I had been given. Now it was midnight and I judged it wiser to let my patient sleep, if he could, until daylight came and I would be able to scan a much wider area. I told the pilot my plan, and he nodded. For the rest of the night I sat at the wheel, too upset to sleep.

Dawn came, and I was relieved to see that the spokes of my last search had just missed the LAD. It was right there near the perimeter of my pattern. I drove over to it and found two orderlies to lift my patient out of the ambulance and carry him inside. I confirmed, by his nod and faint smile, that he was still alive. Three days later I was back in the area, so I took a little detour to drop in on the LAD and see how my brave South African pilot was doing. He had died, they said, of shock and loss of blood.

A letter to a friend
back home. (1943)

"You can tell Gene I performed my first
major operation not so long ago,
I cut a mans leg off — I checked up on the a [?]
There was no infection — His leg is O.K.
~~They~~ We were in heavy action. The Medical
Officer couldn't begin to handle it all.
I told him I that I could do it — so —
Anesthetic — cut it off, clean it, sulfanilimid
bandage it up, morphia; and a drink of water.
Its all over, nothing to it. Shock is usually so
great out here that there is very little bleeding to
worry about. Besides, the character of the wounds
themselves usually seals the vessels. There are m~[?]
abrasions than lacerations —

Westward Ho!

My next move was to head westward into Tunisia in search of my field service company. I had no desire to serve as Captain Young's personal chauffeur and ambulance driver any longer.

I had to advance with care because General Rommel was covering his retreat from our overwhelming forces with an effective tactic. He had put 88-millimeter cannon emplacements at strategic locations, camouflaged or dug in where possible. Each gun had an Italian gun crew, backed by one German infantryman armed with a machine gun to make sure the Italians didn't surrender. Strung out from near the Mediterranean coast southward down into the desert, these units blocked the Eighth Army's advance so effectively that it took special tank tactics by the British to punch holes in the line.

Using the Valentine tanks (a low, maneuverable lightly armored vehicle capable of forty miles per hour), our army managed to knock out some of the emplacements by driving zigzag courses at speed and running right over the gun and its crew. Once past, they could fire back into what was left of the crew, including their watchman. This opened up enough holes for the British to begin moving through. Even so, it took an end run by American Sherman tanks around the south end of the German line to force the entire enemy army to pull back and retreat toward Tunis and ultimately Cape Bon.

I had only one rough spell in my westward safari. At one of the points where the Germans blocked our advance, I had to evacuate the wounded nonstop for over fifty hours. Once the pressure was off, I made the mistake of lying down in the sun, where I fell asleep for a couple of hours. When I was awakened for supper, I felt awful! The idea of eating was repulsive. All I wanted was water. Now that I had found and rejoined my ambulance company, I had no fear of exhausting my own supplies, so I drank my fill and turned in for a long night's sleep in my own ambulance. Next morning, I had a hearty breakfast of battlefield fare that I wouldn't look at now. Oh, the tea wasn't too bad.

Outside Tunis, our company was directed to bivouac in an olive grove until further notice. The vegetation was a welcome contrast to the desert we had left behind, but the lack of activity was enervating. I decided to take one of my friends, "Spook" Wallace, along on a little tour of the countryside. Heading out into the low hills south of Tunis, we passed alongside a field dotted with large canvas-covered boxes of varying sizes. "I'll bet that's an enemy ammo dump," I told my friend. "Let's have some fun!"

Making a U-turn, I pulled over to the edge of the road and stopped. I left the engine running, got my Mauser rifle out from the back of my ambulance, and we crouched down behind the hood of the engine. First, we looked all around to make sure no one was in sight. Then I loaded the rifle with tracer bullets I had "scrounged."

The hood made a good gun support, which I needed because it was a long shot even to the nearest pile of whatever they were. I pumped four or five tracers into the gray pile, and nothing happened even though I was pretty sure I had been hitting the target. Then we noticed a small wisp of smoke climbing straight up out of the side of the pile I had been shooting at. We jumped into the ambulance, and I put the pedal to the metal. As we approached our bivouac area, we heard a distant rumble, then another, and another. I slowed down to hopefully avoid the impression of having anything to do with whatever was happening back there. My friend and I had a hard time keeping a straight face at supper as everyone speculated about the rumor that an old ammo dump had been blown up. Theories were offered as to which force might be responsible. Had anyone known the truth, they would almost surely have considered that what happened a couple of days later was appropriate retribution for such irresponsible behavior.

SURVIVAL FIT

My catastrophe would not have happened if I had more sense than to play at being a volunteer sapper. Our location seemed fine to me, until I discovered that quite a few "butterfly bombs" had been left among the olive trees at the edge of our camp. Butterfly bombs are a sort of airborne land mine developed by the Germans. They are small canisters dropped from planes that do not explode when they hit the ground. Instead, the shock of landing releases a hair trigger that will explode the canister when it is moved in any way. The canister contains shrapnel which disperses with force when the canister explodes, with devastating effect if they strike anyone within about fifty feet. The bombs are painted bright orange to attract the curious, or anyone whose movements cause vibrations that set them off.

These bombs should have been removed by sappers (soldiers trained in bomb location and removal), but they weren't. The situation looked like an opportunity to use my rifle for a good purpose. It was midafternoon, and no one was nearby. I got the Mauser and some regular bullets and took aim at one of the "butterflies" a good distance away. When I shot, there was a loud bang, a little smoke, and nothing left of the bomb. Very satisfying. I continued my target practice for over an hour with a perfect score but not aware of the diminishing visibility as the sun set and I moved closer and closer to my targets.

Finally, it happened. Almost simultaneously with a canister's explosion, I felt a tremendous blow across my abdomen that knocked me backward into a sitting position on the ground. My instinctive reaction was to immediately rip open my pants to check the condition of my genitals. They looked unhurt, but the pain in my belly extended higher all the way up from a small perforation on my left hip into deep in the back of my right side.

I looked up at the setting sun in total anguish wondering, Is this where I'm going to end, out here in this little grove? Then I rolled over in a "sit-out" I'd learned wrestling and crawled slowly back to my ambulance where my friend Spook Wallace was reading. I dragged myself up the open rear end of my ambulance onto the bare floor. Knowing who was reputably the best surgeon in the area, I told "Spook" he could scrounge everything in my ambulance if he could get me to Major Hamilton.

I must have passed out for a while because the next thing I recall is being in a large tent, still on a stretcher, surrounded by other men on stretchers. It was quiet and from time to time one of the loaded stretchers was carried out. I suspected I was in a CCS (casualty clearing station). My pain had reduced somewhat. After a while, my turn came. I was carried into another tent nearby and slipped onto an operating table under a large, bright overhead light. Then someone, probably an orderly, began pushing a tube down my throat in a way that it was blocking my breathing and choking me at the same time. I automatically swung my right hand in a karate chop to the larynx. My chop connected with something, and the tube disappeared. I sat up and said, "If you Tommies had ever done any real drinking, you would know how to empty your stomach. Here, give me that pan!" Someone handed me a pan, and I stuck the third finger of my right hand deep into my throat. That made me vomit right away. After repeating the process, I lay back and asked them to give me the ether. Someone did and it smelled wonderful. I inhaled deeply and lost consciousness on the second pull. I found out later that my chop to the larynx had laid the man out. I apologized but was told it was quite understandable. The orderly had inadvertently stuck the stomach pump tube into my windpipe instead of my esophagus.

Recovery was steady at first, but after about a week, I began to have severe pain in the upper area of my right side. An X-ray showed that a large abscess had developed just beneath my peritoneum. A doctor, having seen the X-ray, came to my bedside and examined my abdomen, manually probing the tender area. He did not look pleased. In fact, he shook his head slowly and walked away.

That night, my temperature ran over 105°. After the very attractive nurse left, a man dressed like a priest came to my bedside and asked, "RC or C of E?" I looked blank and told him I didn't understand. He repeated in a louder impatient tone, "RC or C of E, Roman Catholic or Church of England?" I replied that neither option applied to me, but that if I had to choose, I would take C of E. He left and a few minutes later a, presumably, C of E priest came to the foot of my bed, placed a short plank covered with a dark red cloth across the frame at the foot of my bed, lit a large candle, and proceeded to pray for ten to fifteen minutes. Then he gathered his equipment and left.

Indoctrinated with atheism by my mother, I had no faith in the priest's efforts on my behalf. Nevertheless, his low monotone and good intentions were soothing. I descended into a long, deep sleep after he left and woke up feeling noticeably better. The pain wasn't as sharp and when the nurse took my temperature, it had dropped.

Recovery was rapid after that, so marked that before long I was asked to help carry the heavy container of breakfast food with another man. I did what was asked, but felt clearly that it was not good for me. So I used the cash I had hidden when my clothes were removed and managed to buy and beg some Tommy boots, German pants, and an Italian jacket. Early one morning, well before breakfast, I sneaked out of our camp and headed for the road into Tunis.

Walking slowly alongside the road, I tried to catch a ride in one of the vehicles that occasionally passed. Maybe it was due to my motley garb that not a single car even slowed down. Finally, a Jeep shot past and then braked hard. It backed up, stopped near me, and the driver called out, "Are you American?" I told him I was, and he told me to hop in. As we started up, he said, "It was the way you used that thumb. No one out here uses their thumb like we do."

The American army had recently come into Tunisia from the west in order to help the British push Rommel entirely out of North Africa. My benefactor invited me to join him for breakfast, which I really appreciated. He wanted to know where I was from and when I told him I grew up in Iowa, he burst out that he was from Nebraska. That made us feel like next-door neighbors! From then on, there just wasn't enough he could do for me. Besides bringing me a great breakfast from his officer's mess, he insisted on replacing my "international rags" with his own dress uniform including a pair of his boots (He, of course, removed his decorations and any other identifying items from the uniform). By the time he took me back out to the Post Road south of Tunis, we felt like old friends.

Again I was lucky. I had barely begun walking when a huge flatbed tank carrier slowed so I could get aboard. Rolling back eastward with this group of "walking wounded" I came across my AFS company and reported to our captain, Art How. Art promptly sent me on back to Cairo for transport back to the United States via Capetown.

BACK TO ACADEMIA

At Capetown, we picked up a handful of survivors from a fifty-two day ordeal in a lifeboat after their ship was torpedoed. During the trip home, one of the men told me the only reason they survived was that after their food and water had long been exhausted, they killed the man nearest death and ate whatever was edible. The narrator said he himself ate the liver, which he said was quite good.

We also took aboard thirty-six Canadian nurses, who were more than welcome! The most attractive one of them disappeared into the captain's cabin on our first day out of the harbor and did not reappear until we docked in New York harbor. She was a stunning French Canadian of Indian heritage. The runner-up in our eyes was a red-haired lady whose soldier lover had been killed recently. His name had been David too. I did my best to console her, and we became fast friends. I visited her in Montreal after we had returned from North Africa.

Our small passenger freighter carried a few instruments, so three of us formed a little jazz band. The cannibal was pretty good on the clarinet; we found a mediocre saxophonist, and I, with a lifelong desire to play the drums (but no training at all), did the best I could on the set of drums the ship carried. It was fun, and the other passengers had something to dance to.

We debarked in New York harbor and went our ways. For me that meant reporting to the draft board down in Wall Street (or near there, I have forgotten). I was examined, including an X-ray, which showed a small piece of steel back inside my pelvis on the right side.

I assumed that would automatically disqualify me from military service and was surprised it did not. I was rated 4-F for only one reason: my nearsightedness.

I was relieved to be out of the war but not quite sure how I felt about the fact that I had gone to so much trouble, and almost lost my life, when I was unqualified for military service anyway due to my nearsightedness.

Sort of at loose ends but needing a place to stay while I figured out what to do with myself, I visited my father in New Brunswick, New Jersey. While there, I took a job in the receiving and shipping department of a large chemical corporation just to improve my physical condition. It was also good experience to work with fairly rough-and-ready blue-collar men. At their level, these men took considerable pride in their work. Also, there was quite a team spirit.

With fall coming, my father suggested I get in touch with Dr. Köhler down in Swarthmore College, reminding me that I had respected the man and liked the content of his teaching. I followed this suggestion, and it led to an assistantship under Köhler with free tuition for study toward a master's degree. It also led to meeting and marrying my first wife, who would later be the mother of my first son, who would grow up to become an outstanding civil liberties lawyer and win a unanimous US Supreme Court decision that I had the pleasure of witnessing.

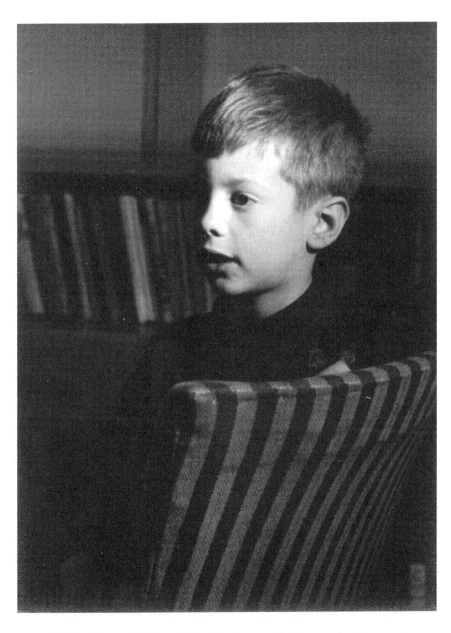

Author's son Richard, by his first wife Gertrude Courant

I followed the master's degree in psychology with a PhD in social psychology and industrial relations at MIT, where I also enjoyed sailing dinghies on the Charles River in Boston. The competition in those regattas was as intense as any I ever experienced, before or later. I only came in first once.

After I received my doctorate, I taught graduate psychology in New York City, first at the New School for Social Research then later as an adjunct professor at Columbia, NYU, the Rand School, and Fairfield University in Connecticut. Teaching, however, was not enough for me. It was not research (developing new knowledge) nor was it hands-on application of things I had learned. I always liked to fix things and solve problems. And I wanted to make more money!

Consequently, I took every opportunity that came along to move closer to the world of business. My résumé was a great help because there weren't that many PhD's around interested in practical problem-solving in production situations involving rank-and-file workers and frontline managers. My mother often called me Mr. Fix It, and I guess she was right. All my life I've had a need to make something work that was broken, not just talk about it.

GREENWICH CITIZEN photo / Lucia Bucklin
Dave Emory fixes a chair in the Senior Center.

ON TO BUSINESS

My transition from academia to the world of business began with three years as psychological editor at the Research Institute of America. They hired me hoping I could bring recent psychological research relevant to effective management into their publications for supervisors in business and industry. For me, it was a great opportunity to work alongside experienced editors. I was flattered when I was assigned to draft Peter Drucker's Letter to Operating Management (after Peter moved on to other challenges).

Not long afterward, I too was ready to move on, in response to an offer from the American Management Association to develop a course they wanted to present to their members. "Executive Communication Dynamics," they already decided to call it. Well, what could I say? The pay, the change of pace (I was to be the only instructor), and the exposure to managers from many organizations looked good to me.

And it was. A year later (1955), thanks to feedback from course attendees to their associates at General Electric headquarters, I joined the General Electric advanced management staff at Crotonville, New York, where I remained until 1961. By this time, my second wife and I had moved to Rye, New York, with our three children and a fourth on the way. At this writing, my second wife and I have been together fifty-nine years, with only four children and eight grandchildren, and plan to keep things as they are for the duration. Professionally, in 1961, I still had a long way to go and a lot more fun to be had, so please read on, dear reader.

Farewell to GE

For a job-hopper like me, you might think departure after five years was to be expected. Actually, it wasn't, nor was the way it happened. In fact, I still wonder if the entire incident was a smoothly planned device to get rid of me without awkward recriminations on my part.

Whatever, here's what happened. A small but very successful management consulting firm was invited to present a sample of their case study exercises dealing with managerial decision making under conditions where a costly crisis has occurred, information is incomplete, probable causes are uncertain, and vested interests are at stake.

My manager asked me to sit in as a silent observer of the class exercise and evaluate its appropriateness for inclusion in our advanced management program. I did, and before the sample session was even complete, the session leader privately proposed that I join his organization as an instructor. His offer was immediate, would require considerable travel, and would pay 25 percent less than my salary at that time.

I accepted. Why? Because the analytical system he and his partner had developed struck me as the most logical, complete, and effective method of problem solving I had ever seen, and the pedagogical method they used for demonstrating their system was the best teaching device I had ever seen. I knew the concepts were valid, understandable, that I could teach them, and that people who used them would recognize they had been helped.

Bea and I never felt the financial loss, perhaps because our standard of living was relatively modest. Also, I have never forgotten how grateful I felt at her instant acceptance and support of my decision.

Beatrice Emery, Author's wife

Time flies (and so does the author-to-be).

Author's first plane.

Learning to Fly and Family Fun

The intermittent schedule of my work as a consultant on systematic problem solving and decision making gave me a chance to think about what I might like to do with my time between assignments. That decision was easy; it was practically made for me by a member of a client group I was leading.

The client was the Port of New York Authority. The individual was the assistant manager of the authority's staff at LaGuardia Airport, well suited for his position by his background as a retired USAF pilot.

Over lunch, during the third or fourth day of the course, I mentioned that I envied the training and experience he must have had because flying a plane myself was something I had always wanted to do.

He leaned forward and asked, "Do you really mean that, or are you just talking?"

I responded, "I really do. I made model airplanes as a kid, made a push-mobile with airplane-like controls, and often dream about flying."

"Would it be worth five hundred bucks to you to get a pilot's license?" he asked.

"Absolutely!" I replied.

He explained, "I have an instructor's rating. To keep it, I have to train two people a year. All you'll have to pay is for the plane rental. Oh, and you have to get up early enough to meet me at Teterboro at 7 AM every Friday morning. Can you do that?"

"Yes! Just call me when you want to start!"

And so it began, not long after the course ended. The first time we were supposed to meet, I got to the airport early, had to wait, and became concerned when there was no sign of my instructor by 6:55 AM. Then I was distracted by the drone of a small helicopter. It came out of the east and settled down not far from where I was standing. My instructor stepped down, walked over with a smile, and said, "OK, Dave, let's get started."

Don was a great teacher. On our very first flight, he let me take the controls as soon as we were up about two hundred feet, and climb steadily to around one thousand feet. Then came rolls into turns to the left and right, holding the bank in each turn without losing or gaining altitude. I was working hard, feeling tense with desire to do well. Don's complete calm was a great self-confidence builder. I soloed in nine hours, cross-country not long afterward and became convinced the Cessna 150 must be the most forgiving aircraft ever built.

As soon as I got my license (plane rental only cost me $350) I went over to a floatplane base at Little Ferry on the Hackensack River and got checked out in a Piper Super Cub on floats. Landing on water looks easy but can be tricky if the surface is glassy. Experienced pilots have been known to crash when the surface looked like it was still twenty feet below their floats.

My entire flight training was like a dream come true. My first plane, however, was more like a nightmare in the eyes of my father-in-law. When we brought him to see it at its tie-down, he just shook his great shaggy head and said, "It's even worse than I thought!" That, even after he knew I had bought it for only $1,400.00. It was a Piper J-5 (a cub that had been upgraded from sixty-five to ninety-five horsepower).

So much for his opinion! That little plane was a real stick-and-rudder classic, especially after I fitted the "joystick" with the cap of a washing machine agitator. Its flight was faultless, and it made some smooth landings! It was ideal for commuting between Bridgeport and Nantucket. At one thousand feet, the Connecticut-Rhode Island coast was my map; if the surf was up at Point Judith, I could drop down and buzz the boys, then hop over to the vineyard and on to Nantucket. No traffic, no waiting for the ferry, no endless boat ride to Nantucket. Total time: 2 1/2 hours.

Only problem: Old cubs are like Model T Fords. Beautiful in the eyes of the beholder but most travelers want more speed, more power, less maintenance.

Citabria to the Bahamas

"Citabria" is "airbatic" spelled in reverse. It is a 150-horsepower high-wing fully aerobatic two-seater capable of climbing out on take-off at a steady 1,250 feet per minute for as long as you like. It has oversized tires for landing on soft sand or deep grass. It is even possible to scoot across the surface of calm water and send up graceful rooster tails (as long as cruise speed is maintained). If you slow down, you get all wet!

The Citabria is great for cross-country travel if you are patient and like to admire the countryside. The large windshield and side windows provide a view like an open cockpit plane but protects you from the wind and propeller blast.

So we sold my first love (the cub) and I transferred my passion to this much newer and more practical plane. I wanted to fly us to the Bahamas, but Bea wanted to visit her niece in Miami and she was not interested in the long flight from Bridgeport to Florida. So we arranged to meet in Miami.

Even though solo, I really enjoyed my long flight down the eastern seaboard. The weather was perfect, my engine never missed a beat, the FBOs (fixed base operators) were friendly, and the time and distance involved made me feel as if I was finally becoming a real pilot. I stopped overnight at a field near Myrtle Beach and reached Miami the following afternoon.

After a day's rest, Bea and I took off for the Bahamas. Heading east out over the ocean, it was a little awesome to get completely out of sight of land. About all we could see was an occasional dark shadow of some large fish in the water below. It seemed a long time before what we assumed was the island of Freeport came into view. As we came closer, two things became clear: this certainly was Freeport, and judging by the waves below, there was a strong wind blowing in from the south. I hoped there was a more-or-less north-south runway at the airport.

Over land and approaching the airport, I called in to the control tower requesting landing instructions. I was disappointed to hear that I was to land on a runway heading at a right angle to the wind, which was now reported to be thirty-five knots and gusting. Normally, I would have requested an alternate runway, but now I could see there was only one runway on the field, with a short taxiway from its midpoint to the office building.

Seeing no alternative, I reduced power, made a short base leg, and immediately set up a cross-controlled slip to counter the wind's force pushing the Citabria out of alignment with the runway. From time to time, I also had to add power in order to pull the plane back over the runway. It was a difficult, scary struggle but I finally put the left wheel down on the runway. I still had to hold the cross controls as we gradually slowed down and settled down. At the taxiway, I turned left into the wind and immediately we were out of trouble.

Much later when I discussed the incident with a more experienced pilot, he made a point that could have saved us a lot of stress had I remembered it: "Dave, don't forget that as 'pilot in command,' you have final say so, even over the tower controller in situations like that."

Live and learn! Or better: learn and Live!

With the Citabria tied down, we did some afternoon and evening strolling and exploring. At the risk of being unfair to Freeport, I'll summarize our impressions this way: Freeport is a haven for compulsive gamblers and alcoholics. It probably has other enticements as well. If so, we apologize for our insensitivity.

Whatever, the air was calm the next day so we left Freeport behind us and headed for Marsh Harbor. Freeport to Marsh Harbor takes less than an hour in a Citabria under normal weather conditions, which we had at the time. From the air, Marsh Harbor is little more than a patch of palm trees with a narrow strip of bare land running down the middle at one end. We had to land there because it is the nearest airport to Elbow Key, our final Bahaman destination. With a floatplane, we could have flown right on over to Elbow Key and splashed down in the quiet little bay at the elbow joint of the key.

Those tall palms lining both sides of the strip were not only beautiful, they pretty well eliminated any strong crosswinds. At the end of our landing roll, a man waved us over to a tie-down near a small office building. Inside, we were quickly looked over by what might have been a Customs official. Official or not, all he asked was what our plans were. When we told him we wanted to spend a few days over on Elbow Key, he said the ferry would be along soon. No one examined our luggage or looked inside the Citabria.

I'm guessing, but I think they all saw at a glance that we weren't transporting anything of interest to them.

The "ferry" turned out to be a twenty-foot flat-bottomed skiff with an outboard motor, probably the best rig for short trips over shoal waters. Our ride over to Elbow Key took only about twenty minutes.

If you want to relax, Elbow Key is the place to go! Small, very comfortable bungalows for the guests, immediate access to wading and swimming in the bay or the ocean, beautiful walks from the elbow out on either arm of the island, and a charming hostess-bartender with a repertoire of beverages that will either relax or stimulate according to your personal chemistry.

We spent some idyllic days on Elbow Key until our personal chemistries and family ties led us to call for the skiff, crank up the Citabria, return to the United States and get back into the business of earning a living.

FAREWELL

Rx for frustration
At the state of the nation:
Mix work and play,
Give love every day,
Disregard decay,
You're leaving anyway,
So what can I say?
We had a great day!

More Great Days in More Beautiful Places

Grade school and college for the kids, management consulting for me, and a professional career as a social worker for Bea kept the Emery family fairly busy for the next ten to fifteen years. Nevertheless, we still managed to maintain our vacation priorities with ski trips to Vermont and summers in Nantucket, where surfing and windsurfing became my favorite sports. Our "stilt house" (so-called by the locals) is right on the beachfront in Madaket.

I thought a few shots of the place and the waves might be a welcome change of pace from my prose.

.

5 a.m. on
a calm day.

Author's beachfront cottage in Nantucket; locals call it the
stilt house.

The family

One picture = 1,000 words

A grandson and our first daughter (his mother) in the Indian Ocean

Jacques
(Richard's
son)

Richard
(author's
first son)

Beatrice
(Author's wife
for last 60yrs.)

L to R: Jacques (Richard's son), Richard (author's first son from first wife), David (the author), Beatrice (author's wife for the last sixty-two years)

BACK TO AFRICA

In 1972, I was a well-paid professional for the IBM Corporation executive development staff. My work had become largely routine, and I doubted that we were contributing much to our participants' future performance. For me, the best part of my job was my daily commute to the IBM Institute across Long Island Sound in my twenty-foot speedboat. Calm or squally, it was always beautiful and occasionally brought me exciting adventures.

Just for openers, one morning in the spring of that year as I cruised into Sands Point Bay and cut back on my rpm's to pick up my mooring and my dinghy for rowing into the beach at the IBM Institute, I noticed my dinghy was listing a little, and as I got closer, I could see what looked like a woman's body in it, sort of draped over one of the seats.

That's what it was—a young woman either asleep or unconscious. As I made the painter fast to the mooring, a moan came from the body and a girl's head turned toward me. "I can take care of myself once we're on the beach."

Thinking how it might look if I arrived at work with a miserable woman and a police escort, I assured her I would not call the police if she was really all right. The reassurance was welcome. She sat up on the seat, told me she lived nearby, and went on her way as soon as we landed.

Luckily, the whole incident had not been seen by any of the IBM staff, but it had been seen by one of the sisters living at the convent on the property next to ours. When I left work that afternoon and started down toward the beach, I heard a loud whisper coming from the shrubs between our institute and the convent. Moving closer, I saw one of the sisters waving. She stage-whispered, "I saw it all. Last night, a big boat with a loud party came in down there and threw that girl into the water and went away, leaving her. She seemed to have trouble but got to your little boat and after quite a struggle managed to get into it. Then she just stayed there."

Weeks later, I told some of my associates on the staff about the incident. Their reaction was immediate, "Oh yeah, Dave, you found that girl in your boat? Tell us another one!"

All right, I will. Later that same year, another unexpected chain of events came my way, and this time there were consequences, some very good and some terrifying.

A quarter of the world away, ten degrees of latitude south of the equator, Tanzania's truly democratic first president, Julius Nyrere, was anxious to see more native Tanzanians in key management positions (mostly held, at that time, by British and German expatriates). Nyrere regarded this as essential for the development of his country, which had a total population of a little over thirteen million and an average annual income of only $75 per person.

President Nyrere requested help from the Ford Foundation in establishing a management training program. The Ford Foundation asked IBM for a staff professional willing to come to Tanzania to design a suitable program. Motivated by the novelty of the challenge, I accepted the offer: two years leave of absence at half pay from IBM, plus salary and expenses from the Ford Foundation, plus a house and car for me and my family in Dar es Salaam. Travel and tuition for our children in a school of our choice anywhere in the world were included.

Julius Nyrere, president of Tanzania at the time, read Dr. Emery's first book, The Compleat Manager, and assigned it as required reading for his department directors in Tanzania's National Development Corporation. The Compleat Manager was also translated and published in France as Nous Sommes Tous des Managers (We Are All Managers).

Flight to Dar es Salaam

KGB, CIA, FBI

The Ford Foundation invited me to take a preliminary trip to Dar es Salaam and spend a few days looking over the house, the neighborhood, and the city where my family and I would be living for the next two years. This foresight on their part impressed me. So did the first-class air ticket with roomy seat and champagne up front. As a private pilot, normally a little touchy on takeoffs, I was in a totally positive frame of mind as the big jet lifted off from JFK.

The last leg of this ocean crossing continent hopping flight originated in Nairobi, Kenya. We leveled off on a southerly heading down over the Rift Valley of East Africa that stretches from just below Nairobi down across the border of Kenya into Tanzania and on to Mount Kilimanjaro, the tallest mountain in Africa. Natives living in the Rift are mostly Masai, those very tall, slender warriors who always carry a double-ended spear. Young Masai teenagers must kill a lion single-handedly to gain tribal recognition as a man. They do it by sticking one end of their spear in the ground, challenging the lion to charge, and dropping down on one knee at the last instant to lower the forward spearhead to the lion's chest level so the beast kills itself as it lunges at the Masai.

Had I known all this at the time of this first flight over the Rift, I might have been less interested in fantasizing about possible forced landings in the open spaces down below. Now the big plane's left wing began dropping, and I felt increasing pressure of my body on the seat. The pilot announced we were over Kilimanjaro and sure enough, as we all looked to the left, we could see right down into the snow-covered crater of the famous volcano. After completing a circle of the crater, we headed eastward on into Dar es Salaam and a smooth landing.

Through Customs and out on the short road into town, I decided to walk. It was quite warm but I was dressed lightly, and it felt good to get some exercise. After just a few yards, I became aware of someone fairly close on my right keeping pace with me. "You are American, aren't you?" he said. I nodded and took a close look at him. Shorter than me, brown skin, sport shirt and slacks, he looked like a man from India. He carried no hand luggage, and I didn't recall seeing him on the plane. His expression was open and not unfriendly.

"You probably do not know how things are for people like us in this country," he said in a matter-of-fact tone. "We have our shops and businesses and a good living, but our problem is we cannot send money out of the country. That is bad because the educational system here is very limited. Some of our young people have gone to Canada, where they are welcome and can get higher education to become professionals. But it is very difficult for them with no financial support from their parents."

He continued, "You are probably returning to the United States soon, right?" I remained silent. "I would like to give you another attaché case like the one you have there. It will be filled with US currency. Customs lets people like you pass right through. We can have you met at any airport by a friend who will give you half of the money in that case. It is worth it to us because we have no other way to help our children."

My first reaction was to doubt whether this man's "friend" would be willing to hand over half of the money, and if he weren't, what he might be ready to do to make sure he got it all with no resistance from me.

My second thought was to wonder whether this might just be a preliminary test by some agency of the Tanzanian government to see if I was involved in some sort of illegal activity.

Finally, it occurred to me that if Tanzania had outlawed transfers of large amounts of cash, there must be a reason for the law, and probably the citizens of this very poor country would be the losers if large amounts of money continuously flowed out of their country. On the personal level, I was being treated royally in an effort to improve Tanzania's GDP. Smuggling just didn't make sense.

So I smiled, shook my head, and walked on, checking to make sure my solicitor didn't follow.

Early Days in Dar

After that postarrival incident, things settled down for a while. I met my Tanzanian boss, George Kahama, my assistant Basil Mramba (who I didn't realize until much later was the coordinator of monthly reports by the housekeepers of all expatriate Dar es Salaam residents), and other officers of the National Development Corporation staff. Mrs. Emery and I were delighted with our large house facing the harbor, the ample yard with beautiful flowers and flowering trees, and friendly neighbors. The house came with a cook, day-and-night security guards, and a chauffeur. As I liked to drive myself, I refused the chauffeur.

Our son Christopher, on vacation from school in Switzerland, arrived and we started surfing in the harbor. The swell was rarely challenging, but it was always cooling and fun. At first, we had the waves completely to ourselves. Later, a Russian boy who spoke some English approached Chris for help getting started.

Kohlia turned out to be the son of Nikolai Krestnikov, the Russian ambassador to Tanzania. Flowers, fruits, and a gracious note arrived from Mrs. Krestnikov, the ambassador's wife. Then we received an invitation to dinner at the Krestnikov's apartment. Another couple, friends of theirs, would be there.

Nikolai and Larissa Krestnikov welcomed us like old friends. The dinner was superb, and the wine and vodka flowed freely. Afterward, the ambassador invited me to join him out on their balcony. Out there, a full moon was rising through the palm trees, and a mild breeze came in from the harbor. Nikolai indicated a comfortable seat for me so I could face the moon and the palms and took one for himself with his back to the view. For a few minutes, we sat in silence. Then, with his hand on my shoulder for emphasis, Nikolai began speaking in a very firm tone, "David, the East-West tension, this competition between your country and mine, is ridiculous and costly for both of us! It brings out the worst in our political leaders and keeps too many of our people poor. Russia's internal economic problems make us dangerous. We desperately need to increase our productivity! Computers are a vital factor." (So far, what he had been saying made sense to me—as a pacifist and an IBMer).

Nikolai continued, "Russia can put a man on the moon all right, but we are weak on midlevel computers like your Model 135 System 360. David, if you could get us a copy of the working drawings for that, you would be striking a blow for peace and freedom!"

I responded, "Nikolai I'm not an engineer. My field is organization and management development."

Nikolai said, "But you are associating with systems engineers in your work at IBM. You could get a copy from one of them."

Me: "Why don't you just buy one?"

Nik: "They won't sell them to us."

Me: "Why don't you buy one through a third party and use that for a model?"

Nik: "We tried that, but after our experts took it apart, they couldn't get it back together!"

Nikolai concluded our balcony chat with a financial proposition: "David, our trade association has ample funds to support arrangements like this. What I have in mind would be enough to take care of your children's college education and provide a comfortable retirement for you and Beatrice. The arrangement would be entirely secret. We would just establish a numbered account for you in a Swiss bank. Think about it! We'll talk more. Now let's join the others."

Back inside with Larissa and the others, I had a hard time keeping my mind on conversation. I knew I would not accept Nikolai's proposal, but I kept wondering what, if anything, I should do about it.

CIA Request

The next morning, I phoned the American Embassy in Dar, requesting an appointment with the ambassador. It appeared that the ambassador was very busy, until I mentioned Krestnikov's name. Then I was given an appointment that very afternoon.

Ambassador Beverly Carter was a very tall black man. After we shook hands, he asked me if I would mind having an assistant of his sit in along with his secretary. I appreciated his asking.

Assuming that Carter already had obtained some information about my assignment in Dar es Salaam, I plunged right into a full account of my previous evening. I quoted Nikolai as accurately as I could and added that I had not said anything about the evening to anyone else, not even to my wife.

Ambassador Carter thanked me and said he wanted "Washington" to know about what I had told him. He also said he would get back to me once he heard from Washington. Washington, I was pretty sure, meant CIA headquarters, so I did not expect any special excitement or urgency on Washington's part over my little encounter with Krestnikov.

I was wrong. The following morning, I got a call from Mr. Carter's secretary informing me that Mr. Carter would like me to come to his office that afternoon, and it sounded more like a summons than an invitation. I was impressed; apparently, my story had triggered one of Washington's priorities.

Mr. Carter came right to the point: "Dr. Emery, I radioed Washington and Washington called back telling me to ask you if you would be willing to keep up your contact with Krestnikov. Washington wants to find out more about what he is after." I hardly hesitated. I realized if I, an American, provided information to Nikolai, the Russian, and also gave information about Nikolai to Mr. Carter, I would in fact be functioning as a double agent. The idea intrigued me. It could turn out to be quite an adventure: Risky? Helpful? Certainly exciting. I agreed to give it a try and to report developments.

Developments didn't delay. A few days later, my wife and I received an invitation arranged by Nikolai to attend a party at the Chinese Embassy (of all places). I never found out what the political significance of the invitation might be, but I certainly learned something interesting and ultimately very useful about Nikolai.

As my wife and I entered the milling crowd at the party, a blond woman with a stately figure like Larissa Krestnikov's came striding across the room, gave me a big hug, and said, "Look, David, tonight I am Nikolai's Marilyn! You know, that popular American actress."

I must have looked puzzled, because she lifted the corner of her blond wig so I could see her own brunette hair. "Didn't you know Nikolai is absolutely crazy for that woman?" Larissa explained. I was embarrassed and felt sorry for this gracious, gifted pianist who apparently felt a need to cater to Nikolai's appetite in this way. We left the party early without seeing Nikolai.

We didn't have any more contact with the Krestnikovs for several weeks, which helped me focus on my sample survey and personnel analysis of Tanzanian business. This seemed fundamental to me as the starting point for designing a relevant management training program. Since tourism is a major source of income for Tanzania, considerable travel to game parks and beach resorts would be necessary. The first step, however, would be a trip to Nairobi to review my plan with the East Africa field representative of the Ford Foundation.

In Nairobi, I found that both the Ford Foundation and IBM Corporation had field offices in the same building. So after reporting to Ford, I went upstairs to IBM to say hello. Lo and behold! The first thing I see on a display table up front is a stack of pamphlets advertising the applications of the very computer model Nikolai said Russia desperately needed. I asked the man at the desk whether these pamphlets were for anyone interested and he said, "Sure, help yourself." I took a couple of copies and examined them thoroughly. There were no diagrams or technical specifications, just promotional material.

After a few days back in Dar, I got a call from Nikolai. He knew I had been in Nairobi (apparently having no trouble tracking my moves) and invited me over to the Russian Embassy. Upon arrival, I was shown into a small room that clearly was not an office. There was a small settee, an end table with a lamp, and one chair. I suspected the room was bugged.

Nikolai arrived, all smiles, and inquired about my trip. I told him I had been to the IBM field office and had picked up something for him. He took the pamphlet eagerly and slowly scanned every page. His concentration was intent, and I felt sure he was speed-reading every line. When he finished, he looked up at me with a serious expression and said, "David, this is wonderful. And David, I have been thinking about something you could do for us, and I know you would like it too." I was having difficulty listening because I had just realized his seeming satisfaction with the advertising pamphlet had to be phony. What he had said Russia needed was technical detail, blueprints that would enable them to manufacture their own midlevel mainframes. They would never get there from what was in that little sales blurb, which left me wondering what Nikolai was really after.

He continued, "David, I know you know a lot about boats." (Where did he get that?) "At this time, our embassy needs a yacht— something in the sixty- to seventy-five-foot class—for entertaining VIPs. They build beautiful boats like that up in Mombasa. You could go up there, pick something like that out for us, and bring it down the coast to Dar. You could take Beatrice with you. She would like that! As I told you, we have ample funds for something like that, and there would be plenty beyond the cost of the boat to compensate you for your time and effort. Just think how much you and Beatrice would enjoy the trip down the beautiful East African coast!"

Nikolai almost had me that time. His proposition was really tempting, so tempting I didn't say no but I didn't say yes either. Quick speculation: might I get away with it if I returned every shilling beyond the true cost of the boat? I just left it that I would talk it over with Bea (who still refused to believe that Nikolai was not to be trusted).

As it turned out, the decision was made for me. Problems with our youngest daughter required a quick trip back to the United States (again generously financed by the Ford Foundation). While I was back, I decided to drop in to see my IBM boss, just to keep in touch. When we chatted and I began telling him about Nikolai, he held up his hand, "Say no more, Dave. I want you to meet someone you may have had in your class over at Sands Point." He got me an immediate appointment.

I didn't remember this member of IBM's corporate legal staff, but we skipped the pleasantries. As soon as I was inside his office, he said, "Dave, I want you to know I am the FBI in IBM, so what's the story?"

I told the lawyer exactly what had happened with both Nikolas Krestnikov and Beverly Carter. When I finished, the lawyer asked, "Did you accept any money?"

I told him the truth, "Not a cent."

He nodded and said, "The CIA had no business using you in that way. Krestnikov is known to us and is dangerous. Your job is to break off the relationship. That's your problem. All I can do for you is give you a number you can use anywhere in the world if you're in real trouble. Wherever you are, we'll get help to you."

That shook me up! How could I shake off this Russian hero tank-commander-KGB trained aggressive ambassador who seems to think he has found a source for information helpful to the motherland? Oh yes, and it has to be done in a way that doesn't make our hero so mad he applies some of his old military methods. That's quite a challenge for a novice double agent. I tried to think if there was anything I knew about Nikolai that might cause him to want to break off the relationship, anything that would make my presence a source of embarrassment for him.

Then I had an idea. I remembered that evening at the Chinese Embassy in Dar when Larissa told me about Nikolai's fantasies for Marilyn Monroe. Maybe this was the weakness I could use. All I needed was a copy of that famous calendar with the nude photographs of Marilyn, a different pose for each month. I would also need a proper gift for Larissa. I found both items in New York City. For Larissa, I bought a beautiful book of large photos exploring the Nile. I had both items gift-wrapped.

As I anticipated, soon after I returned to Dar es Salaam, Bea and I were invited to dinner at the Krestnikov's. A few other friends of theirs were included. After we finished eating, I presented Larissa with the book on the Nile. Then, once Nikolai had settled in his easy chair with the rest of us close by, I handed him his gift. Beaming, he started to unwrap it. As he caught a glimpse of the cover, he hastily bunched wrappings over the calendar, thrust it under his chair, and said at the same time, "Oh! Oh! Let's all have another round of drinks." He did not look directly at me for the rest of the evening.

About two weeks later, Nikolai invited me to lunch at a rather unattractive Chinese restaurant in the commercial section of Dar es Salaam. The place was practically empty. We were shown to a table in the rear, and Nikolai ordered a modest lunch. So did I, remaining silent afterward.

Nikolai made small talk, with no reference whatsoever to his previous proposals or my calendar gift to him. My guess was that Nikolai got the message: I had deliberately embarrassed him as my way to communicate "no deal" no matter what he offered.

I never saw or heard from Nikolai again. Years later, I was told that he died of a heart attack. I also was told that an IBM R&D technician working overseas was discovered, fired, fined, and jailed for passing confidential information to a foreign government. Finally, I was told that our intelligence believed what Krestnikov wanted from me was not working drawings for a specific IBM computer. He just wanted me to accept money or do anything that would compromise me so I could be blackmailed in the future. Krestnikov had targeted me as a candidate for increasing the KGB's stable of informants whenever information they might have was desired. This strategy of informants buried in enemy organizations is not new. It continues today in the military, federal, and business worlds.

Double Agent in Dar es Salaam

In the spring of '72
Little David sailed the seas a'blue.
Round the Cape without a scrape,
Past Zanzibar and on to Dar.

Met Nikolai the super spy,
He invited Dave upon a mission:
Save the world, get a grand commission

Dave was tempted, but reason preempted,
He smelled a rat, and that was that!
The only problem was how to get out,
Nikolai was tough, and might get rough.

The movie star of the Russian's dreams,
Solved Dave's problem without any screams.
Stripped down to bare essentials,
She showed Nikolai her great credentials.

Nikolai seemed to get the point,
But now his nose was out of joint.
He thought he'd try another ploy,
Little David stood firm, declared, "No joy."

ORGANIZED CRIME IN THE DESERT

Information espionage wasn't the only international crime I encountered in Tanzania. Diamond smuggling, recently brought under some control, had cost the country millions in lost tariff and outright theft.

Diamonds in Tanzania were discovered by Dr. John Williamson, a Canadian professor of geology, who felt so sure western Tanzania was a prime location for diamonds that he organized six expeditions down into the desert south of Lake Victoria and finally, broke and sick, he tried once more and found one of the world's richest diamond "pipes" (as these strips of diamonds at or near the surface are called).

These diamonds are very easy to mine and easy to steal. The gathering and sorting process requires a few large machines and lots of manual labor. To control theft, the mining compound was heavily fenced so no one could enter or leave without being searched. The Williamson mine was so far from any commercial center that a large meat- and grain-producing farm was established and included inside the compound. Nevertheless, a steady flow of diamonds bypassed compound controls and Customs for years. Scotland Yard special police were brought in, but the flow continued. It was only after twenty years, when a large reward was posted, that the method of theft was found out and the flow of diamonds was stopped.

The pilot who flew me from Dar to the mine told me how the mine workers did it. Workers at the end of the sorting line pocketed a portion of the diamonds and passed them on to a friend who worked on the farm. The farm workers mixed the diamonds into the feed for the pigs about to be trucked into Dar es Salaam (the farm was so productive the surplus was sent to a meat-packing house in the city). The pigs were trucked alive because the trucks had no refrigeration. After they were unloaded, the trucks were cleaned out by workers who were part of the gang. The retrieved gems were then smuggled past Customs and on to buyers.

The whole story was confirmed by a manager at the mine. It left me with something to keep in mind when considering native resources for management training: don't assume people from out in the bush, with little or no formal education, are incapable of consistent performance even under risky conditions. Also, keep in mind that many very "ordinary" people are excellent team workers when the goals of the work are clearly defined. But be careful; there are a few individuals around who may be ready to sabotage the team for personal benefit!

Final principle: There may be value where you least expect it. Don't turn up your nose at pig shit.

Screams at Ngorongoro

The Ngorongoro Crater is about a two-hour drive west from the Arusha International Airport. However, it would be a mistake to plan on making the drive and visiting the crater in one day. You need a good night's rest and a four-wheel drive Land Rover to appreciate, and be safe, on your descent into the area where the animals live. There are no fences or barriers of any kind down there, just hungry and thirsty lions, wildebeests, zebras, hyenas, snakes, birds, and many other species of wildlife. Ngorongoro is arguably the greatest game park in the world.

To get to where the wildlife is, one must drive down a very narrow, single-track trail that has a vertical wall on your right and a near-vertical drop-off on your left. The total height of the walls is about five hundred feet, which is why no fences are needed down in the crater. The car track is one-way, with exit trails elsewhere.

Great fields of flamingos cover the marsh grass and show no sign of concern as your Land Rover passes nearby along the bottom of the crater. Neither does any of the other wildlife we passed. After a while, we pulled into a small parking spot beside a pond. Another Land Rover with four Italian men was already parked there (my wife, who speaks Italian, recognized their nationality).

On the other side of the pond, a group of about two dozen wildebeests were drinking. Suddenly, so fast she was barely more than a blur, a lioness shot out of the grass near the edge of the pond and struck down a wildebeest as the rest raced away. The poor animal never had a chance. The lioness pinned him down with a big paw on his neck and then paused as if to consider where she would begin her meal. (We surmised the lion was a female because it is known that lionesses do most of the hunting for their family.)

Slowly, keeping the wildebeest pinned on his side, the lioness stretched out her head toward the beast's lower belly and in one mouthful, bit off his testicles.

There was an instantaneous, simultaneous scream from the four Italians in the car next to us. As we both backed up to leave, I tried to lighten the moment: "We have just seen the ultimate implementation of women's liberation!"

My humor was not appreciated.

90

Peaceful Mammoths and Criminal Activity

The game park near Lake Manyara has lots of palm trees, flowering trees, and grass. It is a great place to see the graceful giraffes and ponderous elephants. They both move slowly when feeding, but surprisingly fast when fleeing or fighting. It pays to respect their space. Do not crowd them for a close look, even in a Land Rover.

After Manyara, we headed back to Arusha and on to Moshi. At Moshi, we were warned not to drive down the long descent through the "Switzerland of Africa" for two reasons: It's one of the most beautiful stretches of inland roadway in Tanzania that should be seen by daylight. Second, this is the land of the Chaggas, who are very energetic and occasionally dangerous. We heeded the warning and spent the night in Moshi. Later, we heard what happened to a foreign volunteer worker who refused to be delayed.

He drove on, with his wife and child, until near midnight when he was flagged down by someone who apparently had car troubles. When the driver stepped out to see if he could help, the flagman demanded money and possessions. Fearing for his wife and daughter, the volunteer tried to overpower his attacker, who killed him with a panga (a machete-like weapon). The wife and daughter were not harmed.

This was the only violent crime I heard about during my two years in Tanzania. However, I did get pick-pocketed in broad daylight on Independence Avenue, a main street in Dar. It happened like this.

As I walked along the uncrowded sidewalk, I felt a mild bump against my right elbow. As I turned to see who or what it was, I felt a finger slide from the bottom to the top of my left back pocket (where I usually keep my wallet). I turned immediately to the left and grabbed the shirt of the man I thought had taken my wallet. Then, holding onto him, I swung back and grabbed the one who had bumped me (Both of these men were about my height but thinner). I shook them as hard as I could, and lo and behold, my wallet landed on the sidewalk near my feet. Releasing the man on my right, I scooped up the wallet and walked on, dragging the man on my left behind me.

After about half a block, an elderly Tanzanian came over and asked, "What's the matter, man. What's wrong?" I told him what had happened, including the fact that I had recovered my wallet and was taking the thief to the police. He leaned close and said, "Leave it, man, leave it!"

I knew immediately that he was right. I released the pickpocket, who scampered off across the street, and resumed my walk with some sobering thoughts; I had overreacted at the moment of the theft. Suppose these two had been part of a gang close by or were armed and ready to use their weapons? I could have met the fate of the volunteer on the Moshi road, who justifiably assumed his wife and daughter were in danger. In my case, I was only trying to recover my wallet, which only contained seven shillings ($1.00) and my driver's license. If the old native hadn't come along and I had brought the thief to the police, the incident would probably have been noted by the press, and could have led the Ford Foundation to question the reliability and risk of having such a volatile character design a program to prepare native Tanzanians for higher management positions. After all, making sound decisions in situations involving serious risk is a major factor in effective managing, especially at higher organization levels.

The fantasy of press coverage about our management development study was about to become reality. A well-publicized conference on the subject was held by the National Development Corporation of Tanzania in which Operation Leapfrog was featured. The promises implied in some of the presentations got a big spread in the newspaper. Tanzania's need to enlarge and strengthen its management cadre was clear. Just how to do it, was not.

"Training" was the accepted nostrum, but what kind of training? That is what I had been sent to find out. My first step had been to take a close look at what kinds of business and industry existed in Tanzania. Any good encyclopedia can give you that, but I wanted to see these places up close, and I wanted to see work being done; and especially, I wanted to talk to and listen to the people who do the work, and the people who manage the people who do the work, and the people who manage the people who manage the people who do the work. Of course, even in two years, one survey researcher could only do all this on a sampling basis.

Questions to have in mind during the data collection phase of the study would be the following:

- Is this person effective in his work?
- Does this person appear to like his work?
- Does this person get along with other workers?
- Does this person respect his manager? Why?
- Does this person respect his subordinates? Why?
- Could this person handle greater responsibility?
- What kind of training would help this person advance?

Some significant characteristics of some native workers had already been noteworthy during my visits to the Williamson diamond mines and the game parks. Quite a few more interviews with subjects in different parts of the country and in different types of enterprises would be needed. More frontline manager respondents were also essential for our purpose.

By location, I visited enterprises in Tanga, Morogoro, Dodoma, and several along the coast of Dar es Salaam. By type of enterprise, a small steel rolling mill, a tire factory, meat packing, game parks, hotels, and beach resorts.

Operation Leapfrog Conference at NDC in Dar es Salaam

FINDINGS AND RECOMMENDATIONS

All my observations and interview responses made one thing very clear: the kind of management development programs currently conducted in the United States would not be appropriate in Tanzania. There is already considerable doubt how much and in what ways these programs actually improve subsequent performance of attendees. "Feedback" collected during or at the end of a program is likely to be unreliable and self-serving. Contributing speakers to US programs frequently sound as if their primary goal is to be entertaining (and thereby garner positive feedback).

Tanzania needs to increase its gross national product. To do this, and benefit native Tanzanians, the country needs more good higher-level managers. The best place to find potentially good higher-level managers is among lower-level managers that have already proven they are good managers.

How do you know when a low-level native manager is "good"? Look for foremen whose workers are consistently above average in productivity and have a positive team spirit. Foremen that have maintained groups of people who produce well and feel good about it are the best bet for leadership at the general management level. Warning: neither of these factors alone is an adequate basis for selecting candidates worthy of advanced management training. High productivity without good morale can be a sign of heavy-handed, anxiety-producing leadership. Cheerful morale with poor productivity can exist under a manager who lacks a professional attitude or is just low on energy. Even at the foreman level, managing is hard work.

What kind of training is most likely to help outstanding foremen deal with the greater complexity and consequences of decision making at higher organization levels? I believe that hands-on apprentice-like experience, first under functional managers (like marketing, manufacturing, quality control, etc.) and then finally under a general manager, will prepare former foremen much better than sitting in lectures by outside consultants.

The quality of the organizations in which apprenticeships are served is important. Two elements of particular importance are the value of the goods or service the organization produces, and the character of management in the organization. The better these factors are, the greater the value of apprenticeships in that kind of environment will be.

Finally, I do believe periodic get-togethers of the candidates could be helpful. These meetings could be quarterly, when participants would be about to shift their apprenticeship to a different functional department. A few speakers could be invited to discuss subjects particularly relevant to general managing in Tanzanian enterprises.

The main value of such periodic get-togethers would be formal and informal sessions in which candidates share experiences and ideas acquired during the previous quarter of their apprenticeship. These contacts with information exchange could benefit participants and the country as a whole in the future.

If it proves effective in Tanzania to use productivity and morale as selection criteria for management training and preparatory apprenticeship in advance of promotion, the process could be applied in other developing countries. But one proviso should be kept in mind: this process might not yield the desired results in a nation or an enterprise led by an autocrat, or in a nation under exploitation by a foreign organization of any kind.

When productivity is sustained by force, morale and creativity suffer. Leaders are not respected, and cooperation is more likely to support sabotage than productivity.

Leapfrog's Postmortem

During the final months of my management study, the flow of war material from China to South Africa dominated the Dar es Salaam harbor and the "Tanzam" railroad that ran south from Dar down along the east coast. This was in support of the freedom movement in South Africa and affected the Tanzanian government's priorities. Long-term management development was set aside for the time being.

This shift, combined with increasing NGO focus on nutrition and medical crises, also took some leap out of my frog. Consequently, my final report was quietly laid to rest in the Ford Foundation archives in New York City.

Personally, I profited a lot from the experiences in East Africa. Close contact with the Tanzanians gave me insights into their motivation and capabilities, and into my own unconscious attitude toward black people. It had taken six months before I suddenly realized I was looking at them as individuals rather than as just another black.

Financially, the pensions I earned from my two employers are now helping some of our grandchildren through college.

Finally, the whole issue of climate change took on new meaning for me. In those beautiful game parks with vast expanses of animal and vegetable wildlife, I couldn't help but wonder what would happen to it all as the world's supply of fresh water continued to diminish.

The snow has melted on Kilimanjaro.

A friend at the National Development Corporation in Dar

FAMILY VACATION TRAVELS AND SURFING ADVENTURES

With Operation Leapfrog on hold and my allotted project time about up, Bea and I decided to do some touring before we left this part of the world. We began our Safari Kubwa (big trip) with a flight over to the Seychelles, a string of British Crown islands out in the Indian Ocean east of Kenya and due north of Madagascar. On these islands, no structure taller than the tallest tree is allowed. It is a perfect spot for swimming, sunbathing, and quiet socializing in a green environment; mostly European vacationers are there.

Our next stop was unscheduled. Our flight to Calcutta made a forced landing in Addis Ababa, Ethiopia, near dusk with no landing lights on the field and fuel tanks still almost full. As a private pilot, I didn't like that at all, but the professionals up front put us down safely. We were never told what the problem was, but we did get a free overnight in a good hotel. Feeling like survivors, we slept well.

Calcutta, next day, was like entering another world. Our "first-class" hotel was a barren ancient structure with a single light bulb with no shade, hanging down from the second floor ceiling by its electric feed line. In the morning, we walked around town, often delayed by cattle roaming the streets. No one touched them because in India they are sacred. Shops located in basement single-window sidewalk holes were eager to make shoes, belts, or whatever for you immediately. It was the poorest city either of us had ever seen.

We left for Srinagar, Kashmir, the next day. Our lodging up there was a small but comfortable cabin on a floating dock at the edge of an absolutely smooth lake stretching across to the Himalayan mountain range on the opposite side. Our guide proudly informed us that American Ambassador Chester Bowles had stayed in this cabin when he visited Srinagar. Patting the bed, he said, "You will be sleeping in the very same bed he slept in!" I suppressed my inclination to ask whether the sheets had been changed since the ambassador left.

Indonesia was the last nation on this branch of our trip. We stopped in Kuala Lumpur, Jakarta, and Bali. The surf was up big time in Bali, so I rented a board and "paid my dues" to this famous break by getting some rides and then trying one of the more than double-overhead swells. It closed out on me before I could outrun the break. Result: no broken bones but a broken skeg on the board when I found it after a long swim back to the beach. The owner was very reasonable (probably feeling concerned about being blamed for renting me the board on such a big day). Whatever, we both knew the repair was no problem.

Our final vacation flight was back up to Agra, India. That is where the famous Taj Mahal, one of the "seven wonders of the world" is located. The Taj is famous for its majestic overall design and beautiful setting. However, what struck me the most was the interior tile work of thousands and thousands of very small, brightly colored tiles. The artistry, skill, and energy required for that was hard to imagine.

Back to the United States

My first assignment after returning to work at IBM was to examine corporate staff activities with an eye to reducing duplication of work, low-priority work, and JIC work. "JIC" meant work that was being done just in case some higher executive should unexpectedly pass by and ask what was being done and why was it being done. Asking sudden questions like that was a long-standing practice of top-level executives of IBM. It was a way of showing interest, and an approach that protected the question-asker from being asked questions he might not care to answer or be unable to answer.

After the creative challenge and freedom of procedural design I had enjoyed in Operation Leapfrog, investigating my associates for wasteful activity on their part did not appeal to me at all. Like it or not, the worst was yet to come. I found out from a friend that the IBM Advanced Management Program I used to work in had been moved from Long Island, New York, to Southbury, Connecticut. That meant that after completing the staff study, I would be transferred to Southbury. And that meant that instead of a thirty-minute commute by speedboat to work, I would have to drive over an hour (in good weather) or we would have to move. Now the long-standing joke that IBM means I've Been Moved took on new meaning for me. I decided very quickly; I would not be moved, not with only a few weeks left to complete ten years in IBM and gain pension eligibility. Go ahead, call me spoiled.

Surf Safari to Costa Rica

Fifty-five years old, no physical complaints, kids all either married or working, wife beginning a professional career, modest but steadily increasing financial security, considering future career as psychological consultant to management, but what to do now? Thanks to a friend at Citibank, a probable overseas attitude survey with attractive compensation to start in three months, but what to do now?

Of course. Take my super surfer son Chris and a buddy of his on a real "surfari" from Texas to Mexico and down the west coast of Central America to Costa Rica, hitting every surf break along the way. That would be a dream come true. Chris and Rick were stoked, so I bought a Chevy van and rigged it with bunks like my ambulance had in Africa. Our boards could ride on top or inside if there was a security question.

Our very own "endless summer" began with some small waves in the Gulf at Corpus Christi. We crossed over into Mexico at Nuevo Laredo and drove westward to Mazatlan, where the swell was about head high. Good surfing there. We made it to Mexico City for the night and woke up in the morning to the most dense air pollution I've ever seen. We couldn't get out of town fast enough.

Heading south, we were flagged down by a large man in military uniform standing in the middle of the road. At the side of the road, another man sat in a sedan with the door open and a double-barreled shotgun on his lap. The fellow up front stepped around to our passenger door, opened it, and began looking around the floor. I had been warned about this kind of holdup so I leaned close to him and watched every move. Sure enough, his left hand moved down low behind the seat he was leaning over and released a small reefer. I scooped it up immediately, handed it to him saying, "Excuse me, señor, you dropped your cigarette." I made a point of saying it in a clear, even tone. He accepted the butt, nodded slightly, and withdrew from the car, waving us on as he closed the door.

We had a much more frightening confrontation later that same day. As we rolled into a settlement of just a few houses, five men stepped out onto the road forming a line across it with the biggest one in the center. I slowed down and began honking my horn. They didn't move. I slowed to about ten miles an hour and kept rolling steadily toward them, determined not to stop. When I got so close, I was sure I would hit the big man; he faded like a bull fighter around the left front of our van. Immediately, I downshifted and floored the accelerator.

After we had gone about a quarter of a mile, I saw in my rearview mirror that we were being followed and the follower was gaining. The road ahead rose gradually into some foothills. I double-clutched into second gear and kept the pedal on the metal. They stopped gaining on us, but they didn't stop chasing us. It was getting darker. Their lights came on and I had to use mine, too. The hills got higher and the turns tighter. This helped because I'd had a lot of experience driving in mountains at The Wilds in Colorado. They finally gave up. Later, the boys said my driving scared them more than our chasers.

More Excitement

Puerto Arista, in southern Mexico, is one of the most popular beach resorts in the country. It's a very long, wide, sandy expanse with lots of room for campers, parties, games, swimming, surfing, and fishing. Outside, shrimp boats anchor during the day to unload their catch and rest the crew. The fishing is done at night.

The surf was five foot and steady, so the boys and I had a good session until I dropped in on Rick and got a significant ding on the bow of my board. Served me right. While I was out of action repairing my board on the beach (I carried a repair kit in the van), Chris and Rick paddled out to the shrimp boat closest to us and made arrangements with the skipper to spend the night on his ship working along with his crew.

I had some reservations about this but kept quiet in the face of the boys' enthusiasm and the low probability of anything going wrong. As it turned out, I was the one who had the close call. I rose early the next morning, just to check whether the shrimper had returned. It had, so I grabbed my repaired board and started paddling out toward the shrimper. To my dismay, when I was about halfway there, the shrimper hauled up its anchor chain, started the engine, and headed out. I stopped paddling to see what would happen, but the boat just kept going! Not knowing what else to do, I turned around and paddled back to shore. By the time I was ashore, the shrimper had reversed again and was coming back in toward its anchorage.

So I hit the water again. This time, the shrimper stayed put. I climbed the suspended gangway, and the boys explained what had happened. Sharks frequently come into the harbor when the shrimpers come in. They come to feed on garbage tossed overboard by the shrimpers. When I first paddled out, the captain and the boys spotted a large shark trailing along about ten to fifteen feet behind me. The captain said the best thing to do was to head out, so I would give up and head back to shore. He was right. Had he been wrong, you might not be reading this.

Checking It Out

The Central American Pacific coastline has many very beautiful beaches with attractive tourist facilities close by and thrilling surf breaks out front. None of these surf breaks are great all the time, or even most of the time. Onshore winds, seasonal tidal conditions, and pollution problems all narrow the likelihood of having a good day unless you have a reliable source of information about current conditions. The same holds true for the kind of crowd you are likely to run into on the beach, and the availability and cleanliness of overnight accommodations. Security is another factor to check out, especially where the country involved is very poor or where the overnight facility is isolated.

Chris, Rick, and I certainly were not affluent targets by American standards. Nevertheless, we had some narrow escapes once we got south of the border. It was only when Chris and I reached Costa Rica that we really relaxed. (Rick had split for the Caribbean earlier.) Chris had been to Costa Rica before, knew his way around, and had confirmed the peaceful, positive political and social climate there.

After some good surf at an attractive location in El Salvador, and eager to get on down to Chris's beach house in Costa Rica, we stopped only for Customs in Nicaragua. Maybe the officials there were just having a bad day, or maybe they just didn't like surfers. Whatever, the atmosphere was outstandingly unwelcoming.

Chris the Diplomat

So it was great to get down into Costa Rica, catch the car-carrying ferry at Puntarenas, and drive around the southern tip of the Nicoyan Peninsula. The coast road, heading north near the beach, passes any number of surf breaks on the way up to Chris's.

Once there, we jumped down and ran around the house to check the beach for erosion. The beach was fine, but looking back toward the house, we could see that a Costa Rican family was living there: father, mother, two kids, and a pig. The condition of the place was, in a word, squalor. I was shocked, but Chris, whatever he felt, kept his cool. He just walked over and sat down near the parents.

Chris had learned a fair amount of Spanish during his time and travels in Costa Rica. He spoke to the squatters in a calm, sympathetic tone for about twenty minutes, after which the whole family slowly stood up, collected a few things including the pig, and left. I was very impressed with my son, and glad I had stayed out of the encounter. Even if I had known the language, I couldn't have handled the situation any better than he did, and probably not as well. It's really great to see your kids grow.

Author with son, Chris

Chores, Feasts, Waves

Cleaning up the place, cooking, carpentry, surfing, and sleeping in this idyllic environment was so free from pressure and time constraint that now (thirty years later) neither Chris nor I can recall just how long it was before we headed down to Panama. What we do recall is the hard but fun work we did patching up the footings of his house, the incredible breakfast we had the morning one of us caught a large red snapper (the sweetest fish I ever tasted), and the surfing that interrupted and delayed almost anything we were doing. Our guesstimate is it was ten days to two weeks. Whatever, for me it was worth much more than the costs and close calls getting down there.

Getting out of there turned out to be quite a struggle. The coast road ended just beyond Chris's place, so we decided to continue on the beach. It was nice going at first, but the sand seemed to get gradually softer. I accelerated but our actual forward motion kept slowing until we came to a full stop. We both knew we were in big trouble, and now we could see the cause: the tide was coming up! The surface of the sand looked dry, but beneath, it was getting damp and softer. Talk about a sinking feeling!

Then I remembered my grandmother telling me how they used to have cord roads over muddy stretches back in Iowa. It looked like our only chance, so we got to work. That rising tide was quite a motivator! Chris scrounged for driftwood while I excavated sand from in front of each wheel. We put the boards and branches he had gathered in front of the rear wheels and left the front wheels alone except for scooped-out channels ahead of them so they could roll on with less resistance and in the direction we hoped to go: slightly to the right so we would eventually get to the higher part of the beach.

We only made about four feet of headway on our first thrust (I drove, Chris pushed), but it was enough to make us think we had a chance to get the van out of there if we had the energy to gather wood and dig sand for fifty to seventy yards. We worked like slaves. No whip needed, just an occasional glance at the tide creeping steadily toward us provided all the stimulus necessary.

When we finally reached a point where firmer sand made it possible for the van to advance under its own power, we hopped in and headed toward a small creek. It was shallow, only about twenty feet wide, with cold water flowing over a firm bottom. We forded it, parked on the other side, and without any discussion or hesitation, we both launched ourselves, clothes and all, into that blissful stream.

Later, clean, dry, and recuperated, we found our way cross-country to the Pan-American Highway and headed southeast toward Panama. We were a little curious to see the city and the end of the canal, but our main purpose was to try to sell the van. We had been told that due to the high import duty on new cars in Panama, clean on-site used cars brought good prices.

Neither the town nor the end of the canal was very attractive. Our van was, however, to a soldier stationed at the military base near the canal. He offered us $200.00 more than I had paid for it new; I accepted.

The car sale, the calendar, and my consulting opportunity with Citibank closed-out our grand "surfari." I left Panama City on a plane, and Chris returned by ground transportation to Costa Rica. Little did we know how much more of Chris's life and happiness would take place in that beautiful country, but one thing was very clear: both the physical environment and the social atmosphere had a powerful attraction for him. His positive, nonaggressive yet focused personality brought him friendship and respect from the people with whom he liked to spend time.

High-Altitude Insights

The flight back up north to the United States gave me a good opportunity to think back over what we had done, and what it had meant to me. Besides all the fun and occasional danger, our "surfari" had given me a wonderful opportunity to appreciate some of my son's capacities and perspectives. It became clear to me that Chris's positive, nonaggressive yet focused personality brought him friendship and respect from the people with whom he liked to spend time. Of course, his good looks and physical prowess worked in his favor, but his success in human relationships was, I believe, based on something deeper. He showed a certain freedom in his choices of activities, friends, and personal career that liberated him from conformity and subordination to values that burden many people.

It isn't that Chris made a point of breaking rules. It's just that his motivation, when his behavior seemed at odds with convention, took its direction from his own concept of what made sense and what he would like to do.

Striking a reasonable balance between "should" and self-abandonment isn't easy. Chris doesn't seem to have much difficulty there. I just wonder where that gift came from.

ANOTHER CLIENT
ANOTHER SURVEY

I was invited to work as a consultant to Citibank by the corporate VP in charge of the bank's overseas branches. He wanted an independent, professional to help him define and deal with reported tensions between foreign nationals and American staff members in overseas branches. Since Citibank had branches in the Middle East, North Africa, Asia, and the Far East, the scope of this assignment was large in both time and travel. The compensation was attractive.

My interviews should leave respondents feeling they had helped both themselves and Citibank, and confident their individual privacy would be respected. It was.

In each branch, I interviewed people in positions ranging from department manager down to clerk. Respondents all spoke English and were cooperative. A number of them sought additional time for informal conversation. In two trips overseas, I interviewed about eighty people. They all impressed me as being serious, strongly motivated individuals. Their responses to my questions were interesting and sometimes quite surprising.

Report to HQ

I introduced my report to the Citibank executives around a table with a word of caution: the information I had for them consisted of perceptions overseas Citibank staff had provided in response to my probes about their past and present feelings and experiences. "Perceptions" may or may not correspond to facts, which are deeds actually done or situations that unquestionably exist.

My point was that the perceptions I would be reporting were factual only in the sense that they had been recorded. There had been no checks on their validity by me or anyone else up to the present time. Furthermore, I felt that what I was reporting at this time was more likely to be helpful to Citibank if action on it were not taken until alternatives had been considered. Overseas branch managers not included in the present survey should also be consulted before corrective actions were implemented.

Findings and Conclusions

My interviews yielded some very good news and some not so good news. The best news was the widespread perception that (to quote), "You can learn more about banking, in less time, in Citibank than in any other bank in the world." This opinion, almost certainly communicated among business associates in overseas branch cities, is likely to attract business and candidates for bank jobs in Citibank overseas branches.

On the other hand, for any Citibank employee who might be dissatisfied with the rate of advancement or the ultimate position level he could hope to reach in Citibank, the ready availability of positions in other local banks could cause Citibank to lose some good people. One respondent put it this way: "New York's practice of hiring from Ivy League colleges like Yale or Princeton, giving these young men a few years experience in Citibank and then putting them in at the top of an overseas branch, makes us feel there's a roadblock to our own chances of ever reaching the top."

Another complaint that caught my attention was this: "What really bugs me is that my boss doesn't have the guts to tell me what I'm doing wrong." I probed, "Are you telling me you want to hear bad news?" He replied, "How can I improve in his eyes if he won't level with me about what he doesn't like in my performance?"

It seemed to me this individual had a point.

Unsolicited Opinions and Attitudes

In the course of my work in Africa, the Middle East, Asian nations, and the Far East, I met many very interesting people who not only responded thoughtfully to my planned questions but extended our conversation well beyond what I felt I needed for the purposes of my research. These additional discussions often contained information, opinions, and attitudes that were eye-openers for me.

The frequency and intensity of feeling involved in many of these informal communications was such that after a while, I couldn't help speculating on what motivated my respondents to share them with me. After all, I had made it clear that while no names of individuals would appear in my reports, all information I considered important would be included. So these unsolicited supplements might be regarded as an exposé by my respondent.

I like to think that what probably led people to speak freely with me was one or more factors like the following:

1. They may have had a strong need to tell someone outside their organization how they felt.
2. They might have been curious about how I felt about whatever they had brought up.
3. It could be just conversational courtesy—by showing readiness to chat with less formality.

Whatever, these supplements to our strict Q&A routine did lead me to feel trusted, and also yielded some content I think will interest you even when you've heard it before.

"Why does the United States have such an aggressive foreign policy?" This question was put to me in the course of informal conversation when I was interviewing bank staff in Egypt. This respondent was a charming, very intelligent middle-aged Coptic Egyptian woman in Cairo. She had traveled in Europe and was fluent in several languages. When I asked what she thought should be done to improve our foreign policy, she was ready with recommendations: "Stop increasing your nuclear arsenal. Cut the entire defense budget in half and apply the savings to helping developing countries increase their productivity. Enforce reduction of dependence on fossil fuel.

If the United States did these things, people in the rest of the world would feel much better about your country. People in nations with terrorist groups would be much less interested in those mixed-up individuals."

Clearly, my respondent had done a lot of thinking beyond her own job and even beyond her own country. I wondered if many women or men in Egypt had as broad an outlook. I doubt it. The majority of the population is Moslem in Egypt, and more likely to be impressed by nuclear power than nation building for democracy. Even in the urban areas where groups of enlightened women exist, their number is small and their influence is a long way from being a significant force in geopolitics.

"America, Land of Opportunity"

In Beirut, Tehran, Delhi, Srinagar, Ceylon, almost anywhere I happened to enter into conversation with young people about career plans and locations for professional development, getting to the United States ASAP was a major part of their plan. Often they already had a particular graduate school in mind and the specific business or industry they would be preparing to enter.

Most of these forward-looking young people did not feel that having gone through their local primary education was any handicap to their career plans. On the contrary, they had the impression their grounding in math, science, history, and languages had been better than most young Americans receive. I share their opinion.

"Upward Mobility in Society" is another subject that frequently came up in conversations with young people and with older people too. Young and middle-aged people want it for themselves. The elderly want it for their children. Particularly in India, land of the "Untouchables," the drive to emigrate is widespread and intense.

In India, everyone understands the dynamics of caste (or class) in society. They know that in their country, caste is a framework that defines behavior, channels of communication, and professional opportunity for individuals born into a particular class—especially if it's a low-level caste. Most "untouchables" will die untouchable, no matter what (unless by some miracle they manage to get out of India).

Social class, in some form, exists in almost all societies. The number of levels and the rigidity of mobility between class levels vary widely. So do the consequences of deviating from expected behavior patterns of a particular class. These consequences in the past could range from expulsion to execution. These days, the punishment is usually limited to ridicule.

The United States is far from a classless society. Family wealth, political influence, personal notoriety for outstanding performance of almost any kind, can all be the key to socializing with members of high society. Once entry has been gained to high status level, many more opportunities become available.

Intelligent and ambitious members of static social structures are bound to be attracted to locations and conditions where advancement opportunities are greatest.

Overall Conclusions

In conclusion, I offer some findings from my work that I believe are true in most organizations regardless of their product line or type of service:

1. In all kinds of work and at all organization levels, people like to feel competent in their work or their motivation to perform that work will suffer.

2. Most people need to have their competence recognized by their managers or their morale will suffer.

3. Most people in Western cultures need to feel there is opportunity for advancement in their organization or their morale will suffer.

4. Most people want to be part of a friendly group in their organization.

5. Most people want to work for an organization that produces products or services of value in which they can take pride.

6. Many people's work morale cannot be sustained by financial compensation they regard as disproportionate to their work input. This is true whether the compensation is perceived as too low or too high.

7. Particularly for large corporations, product value and organizational ethic are communicated by the worldwide media. Therefore, sensitivity to worldwide social perception should be a major factor in all corporate planning.

Thanks to Citibank

At the conclusion of my oral report, I handed over my complete file of interview notes. Deciding when and what corrective actions would be appropriate was left to the bank officials. For me, the study had been an opportunity to meet many very interesting people of different nationalities and to augment our savings in the process.

The most satisfying thing I felt sure I had accomplished was to provide quite a few people with a chance to think in depth about what they had wanted to achieve and how they were currently doing with regard to these objectives.

ADDENDUM

ADDENDUM

Dad Gets a Ride

(My sons introduced me to surfing about
6 years ago, in Nantucket. I got the
ride described below off the coast of
Dar es Salaam, in the Indian Ocean. I
was 53 then, and already nervous about
maybe having only 30-40 more years of
surfing.)

Dear Richard and Chris,

I heard it roaring during the night, and knew something special
was up. At 0:30 I looked out at the bay and wondered whether I
really wanted to go out in that wild mess. I could just pass it
up and go on into the office like I should.

But deep down, I knew that if I didn't go out it wouldn't be
out of sense of responsibility. It would be because I'm chicken.
So I pulled on my trunks and put more wax on / my board.

Down on the beach, I wasn't sure I could make it outside. The
sets seemed continuous, with several waves breaking at the same
time and pushing 4 to 5 feet of white stuff, fast. The suds stayed
big and boiling right to the shore, and I had a hell of a time just
getting in. I couldn't tell how big they were, but they looked at
least 8 to 10 feet.

For once I used my head paddling out, and had some luck, too.
After the first 100-yard all-out push, I looked it over and saw
I'd never make it where I was. So I worked over to the right,
where it looked a little tamer. Just as I got there, a pause between sets let me get through where they'd been breaking.

I thought I had it made when I saw several monsters forming
up outside. There was nothing to do but paddle for all I was worth.
I made it to the first one (or rather it made it to me) before it
broke, but the second one looked bad. It also looked about 15 feet

116

high. It broke just as I was going up, and the drag on my legs
and feet felt like it would/~~~~~~~~~~~~~ me/down into the wave, but I
coasted on through. I kept on paddling further out, just to be
sure.

The view from outside was awesome. I'd never seen anything
like that in Oyster Bay, which is usually a modest chop due to
the protective reef. Now the swells were big, smooth and rolling
in well over the reef. The massive momentum made me wonder about
the return trip.

Looking ~~~~~ toward shore, I could see the curving backs of
the breakers with spindrift blowing off the tops, and I could hear
the roar. Shore looked a long way off.

I thought I'd just relax a little. A couple of fair sized
swells went by under me, and then I saw a mountain coming that I
instantly knew I'd either have to go further out to escape, or
take. The highest point was right in front of me, so I decided
this was it!

It started to lift me and I started to paddle. I needn't
have bothered! The curl picked me up and hurled me forward with
a force that didn't offer alternatives. The next thing I knew I
was on my feet, screaming down the vertical-looking wall and carv-
ing right because it felt like if I stayed straight my heels would
be whipped right over my head.

As I cut, ~~~~~~ I
heard -- and felt -- the top begin to break right behind me.

117

Now came the race for survival, and I've never been so scared and thrilled on a wave. I was screaming down and across faster than I've ever moved on a board, and I could feel and hear the break crashing right behind me all the way -- sometimes on the tail of my board -- as I ran.

That's what I was doing, too: _running_, not riding. I was just praying I could stay ahead of that break, and that the shoulder in front of me wouldn't close out. All the time, I was in sort of a steady state of astonishment at the size of the wave. I wasn't at the top, and it kept looking like 3 or 4 board-lengths to the bottom!

The other impression was the speed. My board was bouncing and dropping down that wall so that I was working hard in a deep crouch just to keep my balance.

That breathless race for survival went on for an eternity of maybe 5-10 seconds and then it gradually began to feel like I would make it. The shoulder dropped a little in size, the sound of the break changed from sharp crashing to more of a dull rumble, and I straightened up a little. About that time, the shoulder closed out up ahead so I cut back to the left, timing the turn so the oncoming break whipped me up and back.

By that time, the wave I had run away from had reformed into a docile 5-foot curler that was holding up beautifully in the off-shore. I even dared a little up-and-down as I took the left right into the beach.

That's right: I had no intention of going out again. I knew I'd never get another ride like that, and that I'd almost certainly get clobbered. Also, I could see that Mom was worried. She gave me one of those, "Won't you ever grow up?" looks, and I inwardly wished I never would.

Because I felt fantastic! I guessed that must be what rides in Hawaii are like, only more so, and I knew I couldn't have made a wave like that a year ago. I know I can do it again, too.

The entire experience was sort of a perfect whole: the timing going out, the selection of the wave, the wild run at the start, and the play on the run-out. It wasn't just Mom or work or chicken-shit that kept me from going out again. It was the feeling that this had been a unique, complete experience that I wanted to savor for itself alone.

Telling it to you adds to the pleasure.

Love,

Dad

In my eighties:
This ride won me first
place in the senior division
of the annual Spero
Beach contest at
Nantucket.

133

120

Postscript

February 12, 2011

Yesterday, the world learned that Hosni Mubarak, the detested dictator of Egypt for the last thirty years, had resigned under pressure of massive peaceful resistance by Egyptians in the main square of Cairo. It was a dramatic moment in history.

It made me recall some of the attitudes expressed by respondents I had interviewed in Cairo, Beirut, Abu Dhabi, and elsewhere. Most of the conclusions I reached about people in business organizations seem to apply to people in government. In Egypt, the surprising factor was that even when the level of frustration reached open rebellion, the action was limited to standing protest in the street. No violence by the public.

I think the Egyptian people deserve great respect for their self-discipline in this event. I also think leaders of large organizations everywhere should take care to pay close attention to signs of deteriorating morale among subordinates. Often a chief executive, under pressure for short-term profitability or other kinds of threat to his personal status, overlooks early signs of poor morale or reprioritizes them for his later attention. If the CEO is regarded as a boss who just doesn't like to get bad news, he may not get the information in time to avoid a serious crisis.

Bottom line: in matters of morale, silence is not necessarily golden!

Résumé

Attached is a fairly recent resume, in response to your request. I would like to supplement the resume with a little information on work content.

My most recent extensive consulting work was for Citicorp. The assignment was to investigate American and non-American staff's attitudes towards Citibank policies, practices and management. I was also to identify any additional problems of significance. This work was done on a periodic basis over a 3 year span in the Middle East, Africa and Asia-Pacific regions.

The Ford Foundation assignment in Tanzania was aimed at aiding that country towards its goal of self-sufficiency. My responsibility was to assess management development needs in all major industries, design a program for accelerated training of Africans for top management positions, and install such a program in some appropriate local institution.

My work in IBM and General Electric was primarily in two areas: Design and installation of executive development programs (including extensive teaching); Evaluation of effectiveness of organizational units.

The Kepner-Tregoe association stimulated my interest in concepts of systematic problem-solving. I led many seminars on the subject, worked on further conceptual development, and applied these ideas in consulting on organizational, individual and technical problems.

Recently, my professional interests have been primarily focused on practical problem-solving. What I like best is a situation that presents a challenging problem and in which visible improvement will follow if the problem is understood. My desire for results applies whether the context of the problem is mechanical or human. In practice, I have enjoyed both kinds, and particularly those in which new approaches were required.

If any further professional or personal information is desired, I will be glad to provide it.

Sincerely,

David A. Emery
700 Steamboat Road
Greenwich, CT 06830
(203) 661-0530

122

Résumé

BS in Philosophy, Haverford College, 1942
MA in Psychology, Swarthmore College, 1945
PhD in Social Psychology, MIT, 1948

Employment (Full-time)

Assistant Professor, Psychology, Graduate Faculty, New School for Social Research, New York City, 1947–1951.
Editor and Chief Psychologist, Research Institute of America, New York City, 1951–1954.
Conference Director, American Management Association, New York City, 1954–1955.
Internal Consultant on Executive Development, General Electric Co., Ossining, New York, 1955–1961.
Associate, Kepner-Tregoe Association, Princeton, New Jersey, 1961–1965.
Program Director, Executive and Management Development, IBM Corporation, Sands Point and Armonk, New York, 1965–1975.
(Independent) International Consultant to Management on managerial effectiveness, organization structure, and work motivation.

(Special Assignment) Director of Executive Development, Government of Tanzania (on loan from IBM and sponsored by Ford Foundation), Dar es Salaam, Tanzania, 1972–1974.

Employment (Part-time)

Research Assistant, Swarthmore College, 1943–1945.
Research Assistant, MIT, 1945–1947.
Research Associate, US Navy project, 1949.
Lecturer of Psychology of Labor Relations, Rand School, New York City, 1951.
Lecturer, Graduate Psychology, Columbia University, 1951–1953.
Lecturer, Graduate Psychology, New York University, 1952.
Consultant, Lightolier Corporation, 1954.
Consultant, Ethyl Corporation, 1954.
Consultant, Gulf Oil Corporation, 1954.

Adjunct Professor of Industrial Management, New York University, 1960–1961.
Professor of Management Communication, Fairfield University, 1970.

Publications

The Compleat Manager, McGraw-Hill, 1970.
Executive Communication Dynamics, McGraw-Hill, 1973.
Many periodical articles in academic and trade publications.

Personal

Born: August 4, 1920
Military: Ambulance driver, North Africa WWII
Marital status: Married, with five children
Hobbies: Surfing, skiing, sailing, flying, carpentry
Health: Excellent